How to Become a
MEGA-PRODUCER
Real Estate Agent
In Five Years

By
obert L. Herd
CRB, CRS, GRI

1   2   3   4   5 *years*

THOMSON
— ✦ —
SOUTH-WESTERN

Australia · Canada · Mexico · Singapore · Spain · United Kingdom · United States

How to Become a Mega-Producer
Real Estate Agent in Five Years
Robert L. Herd

VP/Editorial Director: Jack W. Calhoun	**Marketing Manager:** Mark Linton	**Cover Designer:** Rik Moore
VP/Editor-in-Chief: Dave Shaut	**Sr. Production Editor:** Deanna Quinn	**Internal Designer:** Rik Moore
Sr. Acquisitions Editor: Scott Person	**Manufacturing Coordinator:** Charlene Taylor	**Cover Image:** PhotoDisc, Inc.
Developmental Editor: Sara Froelicher	**Compositor:** D&G Limited, LLC	**Printer:** West Group Eagan, MN

For permission to use material from this text or product, contact us by
Tel (800) 730-2214
Fax (800) 730-2215
http://www.thomsonrights.com

For more information contact South-Western, 5191 Natorp Boulevard, Mason, Ohio, 45040.
Or you can visit our Internet site at:
http://www.swlearning.com

Contents

Prologue

As a veteran broker with nearly 32 years in the real estate industry, I have observed hundreds and hundreds of men and women come into the real estate business. Many failed, a large number made very comfortable livings for themselves, and a special group took off like guided missiles to stellar careers that have brought them recognition, financial prosperity, and satisfaction beyond their wildest dreams.

The number of practicing real estate agents is on the rise again after declining for several years. This reversal is largely due to the very soft economy in virtually every sector except for real estate, as well as historically low interest rates; however, more and more of the total business available in any geographical area across the country is going to fewer and fewer mega-agents. Although a large number of these mega-agents have many years of experience, an ever-growing number of them are not the veteran agents you might think but are fairly new to the real estate industry.

What is it about these people that allow them to rise to the very pinnacle of success in a tenaciously competitive industry within a short time while many other highly experienced agents are getting out of the business because they see their sales declining?

I was the top-selling agent in my real estate association my second year in the business, and after I opened my own firm, one of my agents was the top-selling agent for five out of the next six years. In this book, I have given you much of my own knowledge and advice but I have also included personal interviews with four mega-producers so that you can learn firsthand what it takes to sell 30 million to 120 million dollars worth of residential real estate a year.

Whether you are new to the real estate brokerage business or an experienced agent who wants to take your career to a much higher level, this book will give you a working blueprint that will help guide you through a career that you never dreamed possible.

Do you have what it takes to become a mega-producer? Read on and find out.

Acknowledgments

I would like to personally thank several people who were an immense help and inspiration to me in writing this book.

First, I want to thank Eileen Herd, my wife and best friend of more than 36 fun-filled years together. As a highly effective and very experienced office manager and escrow administrator, she gave me much insight into what it takes to keep the mega-producer and his or her team on track and productive.

I owe much gratitude to mega-producers Nikki Mehalic, Russell Long, David Vanneste, and Hugh Cornish, who took valuable time away from their very busy schedules to share with us their insights into what it takes to become a true mega-producer and what it takes to remain there. These people are the true shining stars of the real estate industry.

I also wish to acknowledge Bill Barrett for sharing his cutting edge wisdom with me about what traits the top 50 agents in the United States all have in common. His down-to-earth style of presenting such important information is a benefit of infinite proportions to all of us, and I couldn't recommend his services more highly.

I would also like to acknowledge Brian Buffini, owner of Providence Systems, for his insight into the changing world of consumerism and how to effectively deal with it in the real estate industry. I have personally seen a huge number of real estate agents reap immense rewards from his insight into how to build a totally referral-based real estate business. At last someone has brought sanity to being a real estate agent!

1

Common Traits of Mega-Producers

*F*or the purposes of this book, I have defined a mega-producer as someone who lists and sells more than 30 million dollars of residential real estate a year on a sustained basis. My findings about the common traits of mega-producers come from three different highly reliable sources.

In all likelihood, you will see varying degrees of yourself in the following chapters. If that is true, it will prove one of the main things that I am trying to convey in this book: much of what it takes to be a mega-producer real estate agent is already within most people who make it past the fledgling stage of becoming agents. It is really a matter of refinement, systemization, a desire to be great at what you do, including giving world-class service, and the guts to go after what you want.

> *"It is really a matter of refinement, systemization, a desire to be great at what you do, including giving world-class service, and the guts to go after what you want."*

The first source is what occurred during my own career, which spans more than three decades from the early 1970s through today. I was, at one time, the top-selling agent in my entire real estate association and maintained a position in the upper echelons of that group for many years until I became a nonselling administrative branch manager and regional manager. Much of what I did set me apart and well above the average salesperson. Within four years I had developed a huge referral business and have enjoyed a six-figure income ever since.

The second source is from four interviews that I had with mega-producer agents who list and sell from 30 million dollars to well over

100 million dollars worth of residential real estate year after year on a sustained basis. You can read the word-for-word interviews with each of them in Chapter 12 of this book. You will see, as I did, that they have many things in common, which clearly set them apart from the average salesperson. If you start to use these traits, you will see your own sales soar.

The third source is from a conversation that I had recently with Bill Barrett. Bill is a highly recognized national sales trainer and one of the leading authorities on cutting edge agent production issues. He also works on a regular basis with the top 50 agents in the United States, and he shares with you the top three traits that these agents all have.

When I started selling real estate in early 1972, no such thing as real estate sales training existed. My job as a mechanic for a major airline had just been eliminated and I had been laid off. I had a family to feed, so I was very motivated. I sold my first home 2½ weeks after I started in real estate, and when I closed that first escrow I had $1.56 to my name.

My first manager taught me a couple of valuable lessons. He said "plan your work, and work your plan, every day," and to never go to bed until you had your next day planned in detail. I learned very quickly the value of time to a high-producing agent, and I thank him for that advice to this day.

The next thing that I learned was a must-do was to see that my time was well spent. By that I mean as much of it as possible was spent with people who had an immediate need for real estate services and was not wasted doing nonproductive busy-work.

I also quickly learned the immense value of sustained, consistent mailings to people with whom I wanted to do business, or wanted to continue to do business. The lesson here is that if people don't know you, they aren't likely to do business with you, and if you don't keep in touch, they will forget you, so sustained mailings to a target audience as well as to your current and past clients is an absolute must.

The four mega-producers that I interviewed in Chapter 12 of this book have many traits in common. You will enjoy seeing the similarities as much as I did. Each of them has built a highly efficient team around them, with each team member having clearly defined responsibilities and accountability. Each one is intense about the immense value of their time. Each one has opted to work for another brokerage firm and not open their own firm as they want nothing to do with the administrative duties that are so very time consuming. They all use classy, highly directed mailings to target groups of past, present, and future clients on a regular basis, and they are all strong believers in the "narrow and deep" concept: that is, work a smaller area, but have an intense and extensive knowledge of it. They have other common traits as well, and you will enjoy reading about their similarities when you get to Chapter 12.

National sales trainer, Bill Barrett, gave me the third source of mega-producer traits over lunch a few months ago. After giving a seminar to several hundred sales associates from the company that I was with, he had a working lunch with all of the managers. I said to him, "Bill, you work regularly with the top 50 agents in the United States, don't you?" He said yes. I asked him if he could tell me the three most distinctive traits that these agents had in common. He didn't even need to think; he said "Sure, they are commitment, tenacity, and a willingness to learn from others."

I asked him to elaborate and he said that every one of them is totally committed to a very high standard in every part of their businesses. Everything from client satisfaction to the efficient use of their time to the standard that they and their staff must work at and virtually every other part of their business has only one measurement—a total commitment to client satisfaction.

They don't just set goals and try to meet them; they are all way beyond that. They make commitments about everything that they do, which are set in stone as though they are already done, and then they just carry out the tasks that are required in order to complete them. The word "try" doesn't exist. Their universal mindset is that once a commitment is made, it is as good as done at that very moment.

> *"They don't just set goals and try to meet them; they are all way beyond that."*

They all share a common trait of tenacity. They set their minds on something to be accomplished, and they tenaciously pursue it until it is fully completed. When they are faced with setbacks and obstacles, they figure out a different way to achieve whatever they had committed to; they simply never give up.

These people are the top 50 agents in the United States. They are at the very pinnacle of what being a true mega-producer professional agent is all about, and yet virtually every one of them has a strong desire to learn from others. Ego is replaced by a strong and constant curiosity about the real estate world around them and how they can make it more productive and efficient, more beneficial for their clients, and more fun for themselves and their staff. No wonder they all have more business than they can handle!

> *"When they are faced with setbacks and obstacles, they figure out a different way to achieve whatever they had committed to; they simply never give up."*

2

Getting Started

The Newer Agent

If you are fairly new to the real estate brokerage business, or have been in it for several years but aren't satisfied with your current level of performance, you will need certain basic fundamentals to set in place before your forthcoming rapid rise through the ranks.

You will need to sit down and take whatever time is necessary to complete a *detailed* five-year business plan. This will take hours, and when you have it completed, plan on revising it at least two or three more times before it is a final document. It will be your road map through the journey of a lifetime that you are about to experience, so take your time and do it right.

Remember the word commitment? Your next step is to totally commit to doing each and every activity that is stated in your business plan exactly when you said that you would do it!

> *"Remember the word commitment? Your next step is to totally commit to doing each and every activity that is stated in your business plan exactly when you said that you would do it!"*

You can take advantage of the sample business plan in Chapter 8 to get you started and add to it or change it to better reflect your local marketplace and specific goals, but the important thing is that you *must* have one, and it needs to be detailed, activity-specific, and have completion dates for each activity so that you can measure how well you and your new team are doing.

After your business plan is in place, you will need to assess your current team, if you have one, and see whether you have the staff necessary to complete all of the tasks to which you have committed. Budgetary considerations will come into play here and you should have them factored into your new business plan.

Let's say, for instance, that you are currently selling about three or four million dollars worth of real estate a year, and you have decided that this year you want to increase your sales to 8 million dollars. You plan to do this primarily through target mailings and cold calling in three specific neighborhoods. Two of these neighborhoods are "bread-and-butter" neighborhoods, meaning that they are in the lower-mid price range that just keeps on selling no matter what the economy is doing, and one is a luxury home or upper-price range area that will generate higher commissions but is prone to quiet spells when the economy goes soft.

Your plan tells you that this sustained marketing effort will generate 15 listings for you in the next 12 months and that at least 10 of those families will buy their replacement home through you. You are going to concentrate on generating listings, with minimum time spent with buyers, so you feel that within four months you will need to hire a buyer's representative to handle the increased amount of buyer activity that you will generate. You need to start interviewing now, so take a look at Chapter 5, which talks about building your team, for information on the duties of the buyer's representative.

You aren't crazy about cold calling, although budget considerations dictate that you are the one to do it for the first 5 months while you build the momentum with target mailings. At that time, you plan to hire a telemarketer. Again, look at Chapter 5 and make the decisions necessary to achieve your plan. You may opt to skip telemarketing altogether and just rely on the effect of the mailings. This may take significantly longer to make the desired impact on your business, but it's also one less person that you will need. Chapter 5 has a full discussion about how you pay each of these individuals.

At some point, probably within 3 to 4 months, you are going to need to hire an office manager or escrow administrator to efficiently handle the increase in business in an orderly fashion. This is a highly important step in your new team-building effort, and the timing is critical. If you experience the increase in business that is sure to follow your new marketing activities, you suddenly will find yourself stretched too thin with regards to handling all of the escrow activities that must take place in an orderly fashion. If you don't have someone in place to handle all of the escrow details, communication with your clients and cooperating agents will break down, appointments will be missed, and your reputation will suffer. This is totally counter-productive to what you are trying to achieve, which is a reputation for having a highly efficient, customer-friendly, home-selling machine, so start early on this part of your team building effort and be very careful whom you hire. Again, refer to Chapter 5 for tips on what to look for when you hire this most-important person to your team.

> *"If you don't have someone in place to handle all of the escrow details, communication with your clients and cooperating agents will break down, appointments will be missed, and your reputation will suffer."*

Target mailings are universally used by mega-producers to gain the reputation necessary to become dominant in the various marketplaces in which they work. You will need to get with a very creative and artistic marketing person to have them design the image-building mailers that you are going to use. Don't go crazy here but don't cut corners either. These mailers, such as postcards, thank you notes, team stationery, just listed and sold cards, and so on, will be your only contact with your new target audience for some time to come, and you need to carefully build your team's image with these items.

> *"Target mailings are universally used by mega-producers to gain the reputation necessary to become dominant in the various marketplaces in which they work."*

The powerful effect of continuity cannot be stressed enough here. One of the most powerful forces at work through consistent mailings is continuity. The same message in the same format on the same type of written materials gets noticed much sooner and much more effectively by the public

> *"One of the most powerful forces at work through consistent mailings is continuity."*

than off-and-on mailings of completely different things in a different written format. Keep it classy, simple, and always the same.

If you are working for another company, you will need to meet with their marketing department or the broker or branch manager to see what guidelines or boundaries they have and with which you need to work. Many companies have some really classy marketing pieces that you can just tap into while others have very little to offer. Be sure to investigate this issue very early on to allow for the time necessary to develop and print whatever marketing pieces you will need on a regular basis.

At this point, I would like to give you a word of caution. Everyone has their own favorite radio station; it's station WIIFM, What's In It For Me? When you develop marketing pieces that will go out to the public, be very careful that they do not just state a feature about you or your team without tying it to a benefit to the consumer who receives it. Real estate agents spend millions of dollars every year advertising themselves as being "number one" in a certain neighborhood, an "area specialist," or making statements about their professional designations, without ever telling the consumer what the benefit of those things are to the consumer, and the entire message and all the money spent is wasted. For instance, see how you would feel about the difference in these two statements if you were a consumer about to list your home. "I'm number one in your neighborhood" versus "I'm the most effective agent specializing in your neighborhood because my extensive marketing program gets homes sold faster and closer to the asking price. Please call me for details."

> *"When you develop marketing pieces that will go out to the public, be very careful that they do not just state a feature about you or your team without tying it to a benefit to the consumer who receives it."*

Can you see how tying a benefit to the feature and then using a call to action will be more effective in getting the recipient of your mailings to call you?

When you have your materials and support staff in place, it's time to start building your image to the public. Carefully follow your business plan each and every day and stay within your budget. At this point in your career, cash may be king, and you will want to use it very carefully.

As you gain market share in the community and the higher profile that comes with it, you will be contacted by many different salespeople wanting to sell you everything from additional Web sites to refrigerator magnets. You will have times when you start to close several escrows at once and feel flush with cash. Don't let this sway you from the good business sense that you used when you created your business plan; just stick to it and build your cash reserves. As you build your team, you will sometimes have the usual growing pains that come with too many staff to pay with too few escrows. This is a balancing act that will last from several months to more than a year, so retain all cash reserves that you can and spend money only within the boundaries set by your business plan.

Be prepared to revisit your business plan along the way at regular intervals and make adjustments. Each year should build exponentially on the success of the previous one. Face your failures honestly and learn and grow from them as well. Every high achiever has had his or her share of failures along the way; it's called controlled growth.

> *"Face your failures honestly and learn and grow from them as well."*

The Experienced Agent

You are a different breed. You have been around for several years, and you have a very accurate sense of the marketplace. You already are doing 8–15 million dollars worth of sales every year and probably have at least one or more assistants in place. You earn a very consistent six-figure income, and yet you know that you have what it takes to go to a much higher level, in many cases to a seven-figure income.

A careful analysis of your existing business plan is as critical for you as it is for the newer agent—maybe more. Because you earn more than the newer agent does, your time is worth more on an hourly basis. This also means that mistakes and time wasted are more costly to you than to the newer agent. A good, solid business plan, often revisited, will really help you to stay very focused and highly productive, so start there.

Does your current business plan include the activities that will create the built-in growth to which you now aspire? How big do you want to get? This question is critical as it dictates just about every area of your current and future operation.

If you want to grow your business by several million dollars worth of sales volume each year, you automatically have one of three options available to you. You either need to keep your staff relatively the same size and dramatically increase your average sales price, keep doing what you are doing and add more staff to help you do it more effectively, or a combination of both.

In Chapter 12 you will see that Russell Long and Hugh Cornish focused on a higher sales price with minimal staff increases while Nikki Mehalic opted for additional staff to do what she does even better, especially handling the large subdivisions that she markets. David Vanneste did both by becoming dominant in inner-city Minneapolis and then moving to luxury lakefront homes while maintaining what he had already created by adding staff.

The issue here is to make that key decision first and then build your new business plan around it. The new plan should state clearly, how, when, and where you are going to expand or grow your business. Give a lot of thought to this. Make your plan and then re-make it some more until you are very comfortable with it. Then have someone close to you, such as your spouse or your existing team, critique it. You will be amazed at how they can find the slightest flaw for you and help you to perfect your plan.

When you have a 5-year plan you can start to evaluate your staffing needs, your financial commitments to people as well as to materials, equipment, and other costs. It's probably a good time to evaluate the image of your team as well. Is it time for a change, or is there a need to reinforce the one that is already in place?

Like the newer agent, if you decide that it is time for a remake or an update to your public image, you will need to get with someone who is creative and who will help you to carefully transition your team while maintaining the continuity of the reputation that you have already achieved.

If your updated business plan dictates that you add licensed people to your staff, then the next decision is whether to hire someone brand new or newer or try to hire a very experienced person. The newer agents are usually your best recruits as they are not as set in their ways and are more trainable. They will not demand the higher monetary rewards that more experienced agents usually seem to ask for either. If your new plan calls for you to enter new territory, such as subdivision sales, builder "spec" homes, land or subdivision lot sales, and so on, then you are better off to negotiate something acceptable with an agent who is specialized in that particular field.

> *"The newer agents are usually your best recruits as they are not as set in their ways and are more trainable."*

Be very careful about who you hire. This is not a time to be someone's benefactor. If you have a close friend who is licensed, such as an office mate or an agent with whom you have been close over the years or even a family member, he or she may or may not be the right person for a particular role on your new team, and if you hire them and they don't perform up to the standard that you want, it will hurt both your team's performance and your friendship.

Let your business plan dictate the speed at which you conduct your new activities. This will help you to pace yourself financially and act as a barometer of your progress in attaining market share in your new markets.

> *"Let your business plan dictate the speed at which you conduct your new activities."*

An example for an experienced person to consider is that you are currently working with three custom home builders who do all of their sales through you, and you want to expand the number of builders with whom you work so that you achieve 8 million dollars in additional listings and sales from that source.

Your research shows you that your average sales price from the existing builders is $520,000. This means that you will need about 16 additional listings from that source. You need to ask yourself the following questions:

- Are there 16 additional listings out there in my marketplace to be had?

- How can I get my existing builder-clients to step up production?

- Does the current economic climate support increased production?

- Who are the other builders in my marketplace?

- How can I get to know the other builders in my marketplace?

- Are there organizations that I can join to get me better exposure to these builders?

- Will my existing builder-clients get angry if I take on any new ones?

As you can see, a logical thought process takes place to investigate, analyze, and implement a strategic plan for entry into, or to obtain an increased market share of any given area of real estate. This is known as the feasibility study phase, and you must start here every time you want to expand your business.

3

Transitioning from General Sales to Niche Marketing

Firmly Establishing Your Base Income First

Niche marketing means exactly that—marketing to a small segment of a larger entity. I have met only a handful of mega-agents who don't have a very large and highly focused presence in a smaller segment of the general real estate community; the ones who aren't "narrow and deep" have something else that they do regularly that clearly sets them apart from the average agent. As an example, a terrific agent whom I know in Tucson, Arizona, who consistently closes more than 100 escrows a year is a disciplined cold-caller. He gets listings in all price ranges and covers a broad spectrum of the Tucson housing market; however, he is very highly disciplined about the time that he spends cold-calling. He does it at the same time for the same amount of time on the same days every week. He related to me a while back that he calculated his income divided by the number of hours that he cold-called and that he makes in excess of $4,000 per hour while cold-calling.

"If you are like most newer real estate agents, you have somewhere between little and almost no cash reserves. Hiring a team and cranking up an expanded business takes money, so what do you do?"

This is an example of a deviation from the "narrow and deep" concept found in most mega-producers; however, the consistency with which he does it is an effective equivalent to the narrow and deep practice.

If you are like most newer real estate agents, you have somewhere between little and almost no cash reserves. Hiring a team and cranking up an expanded business takes money, so what do you do?

The best advice that I can give you is to keep doing what you are doing effectively but do more of it. Live as frugally as you can, start to save the excess cash generated by your increased efforts, and begin to build the working capital that you will need for your expansion. Other faster methods are available to you, such as an equity loan against your home or other real estate, Small Business Administration loans through your local bank, the sale of stock or other assets, and loans from family and friends, just to mention a few. Be especially careful about loans from family or friends as these are very sensitive and can create relationship problems if you don't pay them back exactly as promised.

The most important point to understand here is that you must increase your overall level of money-making activities until you have a sustained increase in your income level. Then, and only then, are you ready to go to the next level and start to build your team.

If you are already an experienced real estate agent and you have a good market presence and sufficient cash reserves as dictated by your business plan, then you can start to plan your transition to a niche market of your choosing.

Planning and Analysis

Your first step is going to be to decide what niche market you want to dominate; and remember, the key word here is *dominate*.

Do you want to totally dominate the luxury home market, several high volume neighborhoods in your town, the new home subdivision market, lake front properties, the builder spec home market, land sub-division sales, apartment house sales and exchanges, or any of the other types of niche markets?

As you can see, you can choose from a tantalizing variety of niche markets. Your previous experience as a real estate professional probably will come into play here as you already will have found some areas that you excel in, and you may want to give a lot of thought to merely expanding those; however, if you are the adventurous type, this is an excellent time to venture into new territory as long as you do your research first. See Chapter 2 for an example of how to conduct a feasibility study of a niche market in order to see whether or not it would be profitable for you to do so.

Whatever niche market you choose, you will need to go "narrow and deep" immediately; that is, you will need to immerse yourself in learning everything that there is to learn about the new market. You will need to earn a high degree of credibility as quickly as possible so that you are on a very comfortable level of communication with the potential clients and customers whom you will encounter in this new arena.

> *"You will need to immerse yourself in learning everything that there is to learn about the new market."*

You must do some careful planning and analysis and incorporate it into your business plan in order for you to be as effective as you can be and not waste your time and financial reserves.

After you have decided on your new niche market, take the time to carefully analyze several important things about it. You will need to know the total amount of business available in your market area from this particular source of business. You also will need to research who the existing dominant players are, if any, so that you know who your competition is and how they work. As an example, several socially well-placed agents always seem to dominate the luxury home market in any given area. Do you have what it takes to penetrate that market and get enough of that business to make the effort worth your while? Don't let your ego get in the way of good, sound analysis here as it could hurt you financially.

Another example is the builder subdivision market. Land is becoming scarce in many urban areas today, and the builders are being forced to move farther and farther away from the central urban areas. If you are going to pursue this niche market, are you willing to travel the distance required to lead the marketing efforts of these new, but somewhat remote sites, and if so, how will doing so diminish your effectiveness elsewhere? (Read David Vanneste's interview in Chapter 12 for some good insight into this issue.)

The most effective method of planning and analysis that can be done here is to first decide on a new market, research how big that market is, analyze the competition, and ask yourself a lot of questions about what it will take to enter that market, create a compelling marketing plan to become dominant, and maintain your dominance. This is best done in writing at each step so that you can sit down somewhere quiet and analyze each step as a go or no-go along the way.

If your analysis shows you that an area that you are interested in is over saturated with other agents for the amount of overall business to be had, don't be afraid to pass it by and look for another one.

Gradually Transitioning to a Niche Market

When you have done your homework and have found a niche market that is both viable and attractive to you, it is time to implement your plan. This is best done by a gradual transition away from the general real estate market.

You already have found some degree of success, and you should maintain it while you make your narrow and deep transition so that your income doesn't decline abruptly. The best way to make this happen is to time block activities in your appointment book or planner.

"You already have found some degree of success, and you should maintain it while you make your narrow and deep transition so that your income doesn't decline abruptly."

Every good real estate agent uses some type of appointment scheduler or daily planner to schedule daily activities as efficiently as possible. You will need to start to block out time periods of from one to three hours a day in your appointment book to conduct activities that are geared toward increasing your knowledge of, and your dominance in, your new niche market. If you start small and then expand in 1-hour increments as the need dictates, you will find that you are replacing your general real estate market income with niche market income as you go along, and minimal reduction of your income occurs during this transitional period. This is a time to have patience and concentrate on sticking to your business plan. You will surely have times when you will get a prized new niche market listing or a great new niche market buyer and will start to think, "Hey,

"One of the highest values of having a business plan is that it will help you to stay on track and not get too aggressive about your transition."

I've arrived; it's go-for-it time." Don't make that mistake. Have patience, stay with your plan, and take your time. One of the highest values of having a business plan is that it will help you to stay on track and not get too aggressive about your transition.

Expanding Your Market Presence

As your effectiveness increases in your niche market and your business begins to grow, you should begin to think about duplicating yourself for even greater market penetration. This will necessitate hiring some type of help if you haven't already. You will need to decide whether your business is served best by hiring a licensed assistant to take care of the ever-growing paperwork and other details that take way too much of your time, a licensed buyer's representative, or both. You will need both at some point, but the licensed assistant is probably the best one to hire first.

"If you don't have an assistant, you are one." This is far truer than most of us would like to admit, but with the ever-increasing paperwork associated with each new escrow and the ever growing amount of other details that are involved in marketing each new listing, such as keyboxes, signs, advertising, and Web site ads; presenting offers, *"If you don't have an assistant, you are one."* keeping flyer bins full, and a host of other things, the licensed assistant is almost a given if you don't want to drive yourself crazy. You, as an upcoming mega-producer, shouldn't be doing $8.00 an hour work; it's simply a loss-leader for you as it takes away from your time as the rain-maker or business developer.

You obviously picked whatever your niche market is because you like working in that arena, and your goal is to be free to do more and more of it. To accomplish that, you are going to have to delegate as much of life's daily tasks as you can to someone else. Keep that in mind as you hire your assistant. He or she should have an excellent work ethic, exceptional people and phone skills, and complement you and your style of doing business.

Don't rush into hiring someone just to get the chore past you; you could pay dearly for that mistake. Your gut reaction will be one of your best guides in this matter if you listen to it. While you are interviewing each candidate, keep asking yourself the following questions: "Can he or she handle the stress?" "Will he or she represent me the way that I want?" "Is he or she committed to the job, or will I lose him or her to being an agent?" "Do I even like him or her?" You should have a written interview information sheet for candidates to fill out before you interview them. Ask all of the questions that

"Don't rush into hiring someone just to get the chore past you; you could pay dearly for that mistake."

you are concerned about on the sheet and review it prior to talking with each one but be careful not to ask any questions that violate the Equal Employment Opportunity Act. I have provided a sample interview sheet in the Business Plan section of this book.

After you think that you have found a good person, be very sure to ask for and personally check his or her references. I have always found that asking his or her prior employer "If I find that I can't use him, should I send him back to you?" gets me some real answers instead of politically correct ones.

When you are satisfied that you have found the right person, you will have to negotiate salary and benefits, if any. If you have any interest during the interview, ask the candidate what he or she currently is making and what she or he expects to achieve in the new position. For a detailed job description of a licensed assistant, please see Chapter 5.

This is a good time to address the issue of unlicensed assistants. In my opinion, an unlicensed assistant has very little place in the real estate business. I don't know of any state that allows an unlicensed person to conduct real estate related activities with the public without a real estate license, and if your assistant is not licensed, you are just asking for trouble. Besides the state regulations issue, a credibility issue exists as well. Your assistant will be in close contact with your clients and customers during an escrow, and

"Your assistant will be in close contact with your clients and customers during an escrow, and having a license is fundamental to knowledge and credibility."

having a license is fundamental to knowledge and credibility.

This is obviously your call as many states allow the limited use of unlicensed assistants, but if you really think it over, why would you not mandate that all of your team be licensed as a standard of care?

Now that you have your new assistant taking care of your escrow work and other "back room" activities, you are free to expand your presence in your market. You can accomplish this in several ways. One way is to hire one or more buyer's representatives, and the other way is to hire a telemarketer or cold-caller.

The primary responsibility of the buyer's representative, or buyer's rep, as they are commonly known, is to receive buyer referrals from you and sell them a home on your behalf. Many variations of this exist, but both you and they need to be very focused on their primary responsibility, which is receiving buyer referrals from you and converting them into new buyer controlled escrows. Some mega-agents will combine this with several of the off-site tasks of the licensed assistant, such as flyer maintenance at your listings, replacing sign-in sheets, putting on and taking off keyboxes, and things of that nature, which the licensed assistant would have to leave the office to do. When you hire a buyer's rep, you may want to have him or her do some of these tasks in order to maximize their efficiency for you and to keep your payroll to a minimum; however, as you and they get busier and busier you will want to separate these tasks and have your buyer's rep perform only buyer-related tasks on your behalf. As you grow your business, you should be looking to add more buyers' reps. You are going to have to be very aware of how busy your first buyer's rep is in order to determine when to add the second and subsequent reps. Don't rely on the reps to tell you when they are too overloaded, as they are paid primarily on commission, and the "more is better than less" attitude will certainly prevail to one degree or another with each of them. They would each be happier with too many buyers to handle, even at your expense, than too few buyers as this would tend to diminish their incomes.

If you are after more listings, and you should be, then you will need to consider hiring either someone to produce and mail all of your direct mail pieces and/or someone to telemarket or cold-call for you in order to generate more listing appointments.

I found it very interesting that none of the mega-producers that I interviewed in Chapter 12 used a telemarketer, nor did any of them do any kind of personal cold-calling. It is noteworthy though, that all of them spend a great deal of time keeping in touch with past clients through personal calls and consistent mailings.

Properly and professionally done, I have found cold-calling to be a highly effective method of building a listing inventory and market share in any given area, no matter what the price range, but keep in mind that none of the mega-producers that I interviewed use that technique.

If you hire a telemarketer, that person should practice and role play with you until he or she is poised and polished and has the ability to represent you very well to everyone; after all, they *are* you to the consumer. A telemarketer's message should be short and sweet, both for efficiency and for consumer comfort.

A script should go something like this:

"Hi, Mr. Jones?"

"Yes."

"Hi. Mr. Jones, my name is Joe Agent, and I'm calling on behalf of Bob Herd with Coldwell Banker; do you have a minute to help me?"

"I guess so."

"Thank you. Bob specializes in home sales in your neighborhood somewhat and always has people interested in buying there. He asked me to call you to see whether you and your wife may have any interest in selling your home in the next three months to a year."

"No, not right now."

"That's fine, Mr. Jones; if you ever have any real estate questions we hope that you will consider us a real estate resource and call on us when you need us. May I leave our phone number with you?"

> "I guess so."
>
> "Thank you for your time, Mr. Jones; good bye." (Always let the person who was called hang up first.)

The preceding script is only one example of a short, nonconfrontational script that may be used by your telemarketer to get you listing appointments. On average, about 4 to 6 people out of every 100 have an immediate need for your services. Although that doesn't sound like very high odds, I took my own company from new to a 29 percent market share in Daly City, California, in only 18 months doing exactly that. When telemarketing is done consistently and tactfully, it is very effective and produces lots of business for you. Please see Chapter 5 for a detailed explanation of the duties and compensation of a professional telemarketer.

"On average, about 4 to 6 people out of every 100 have an immediate need for your services."

After you have employed one or more buyers' reps, and possibly at least one telemarketer, you will find that they very soon get busy showing property, writing offers on your behalf, and obtaining listing appointments for you. You will soon find yourself busy going from one appointment to another presenting offers and taking listings. When this starts to take up much of your time, you will know that you have "arrived" as a mega-producer. From then on, it is simply a matter of good business decisions on your part and where you want your business to go that will be the deciding factors about how many people you hire.

Another way to expand your market presence is to get involved in a regular and consistent mailing program to your target audience. This is not something that you can dabble at; you will need to be very consistent about this in order to be effective, or you quickly will lose your presence to the recipients of your mailings. "Out of sight, out of mind" is definitely the operative phrase here.

It will be interesting for you to note in Chapter 12 that every one of the mega-producers that I interviewed does extensive and consistent mailings to a highly-targeted audience. It is not something that you can try a few times and judge its effectiveness. It takes time for you to become a brand name to your target audience, and you must have faith in the system and do it on a very regular basis, or you will not be successful at it. Have faith; it really works!

Every piece that you mail should have your picture on it; this fosters familiarity with you whether the recipient of your mailings has ever met you or not. You must also be very consistent in the format of what you mail. All of your mailings should have the same look and a similar format. People will come to identify your mailings with you as an overall quality piece of work and will think of you and the services that you offer the same way.

> *"If you send what are obviously cheap materials out to your audience, then that is exactly how they will perceive what you will use to market their most precious asset for them as well, and that is not good!*
>
> *Every piece that you mail should have your picture on it."*

Don't be lavish but don't use inferior quality pieces in your mailings. Many of the people in your target audience will have never met you and will only have your mailings and possibly one or more telephone calls from you or your telemarketer to determine the overall quality of what you are all about. If you send what are obviously cheap materials out to your audience, then that is exactly how they will perceive what you will use to market their most precious asset for them as well, and that is not good!

In Chapter 12, you will read with interest how David Vanneste started with a very focused mailing campaign to the inner-city Minneapolis area, built a significant market share for himself, and used consistent mailings to continue to dominate that area and its sure-fire income while he moved on to lakefront properties and enhanced his business with a major market share in that area as well. He still maintains both markets several years later through consistent quality mailings. Nikki Mehalic is a daunting and formidable force in Oro Valley, a northern suburb of Tucson. She has a huge market share and maintains it through consistent quality mailings to a large segment of the Oro Valley community.

The message here is that you need to start to market yourself and your team through consistent quality mailings and/or the use of one or more telemarketers, and you need to keep it up as long as you wish to remain the dominant force in your area. The extent of your market dominance and your income is determined only by the quality and size of your mailings and the team that you build.

Learn, Learn, and Learn!

Niche marketing is about the narrow and deep concept; that is, you work a smaller area, but you learn literally everything that there is to know about it. Over time, this builds a very high degree of credibility among the residents of that area who are likely to do business with you. You learn who the builders are or were and what new subdivisions are currently being built or are in the planning process through the local city or county government systems; what property condition issues such as roof or plumbing replacements are coming up regularly in certain subdivisions; where the shopping centers are located and the major tenants that occupy them; learn all about the school systems, where they are and how they are rated. You should have a keen knowledge of property values in every subdivision in your niche market.

"Niche marketing is about the narrow and deep concept; that is, you work a smaller area, but you learn literally everything that there is to know about it."

While we are on the subject of credibility, I would like to mention the professional designations that are available through the National Association of REALTORS®. If you think about it, our product is really knowledge. We don't sell real estate, the sellers do. We sell the knowledge that is necessary for buyers and sellers to have in order to reach an agreement for the sale and purchase of real estate. The Accredited Buyer Representative (ABR) course, the Certified Residential Specialist (CRS) designation courses, the Certified Commercial Investment Member (CCIM) designation courses, and the Land Institute courses are all excellent ways to gain knowledge that is critical to your success as well as increase your credibility to your clients and customers. I recommend the courses highly.

4

Marketing and Advertising

Understanding the Difference between Marketing and Advertising

Marketing is about brand name recognition, period. It is about creating the same connection between your name and real estate as between Coca-Cola and soda pop.

Advertising is about selling, or asking the customer to buy a very specific product, such as a particular home or a lot in a new subdivision.

"Marketing is about brand name recognition, period."

Blurring the lines between the two can be very easy, and if you do, you run the risk of spending a lot of money trying to get a certain message to the public that will be nearly or completely lost on them; here is an example of the difference:

"Rancho Sauharita—the place for active adults" is a marketing-oriented statement. It is geared toward getting someone interested enough in the community to drive there and see what it is all about, but it is not advertising.

"Rancho Sauharita's finest lake-front home is now for sale. 123 Lakefront Drive just became available for prospective buyers. Don't miss your chance to own this wonderful three bedroom lake-front home. Call Bob Herd at 520-240-2403 for an appointment today." This is an example of advertising that is designed to get specific buyers to call you about a specific product.

Marketing

Your tenure in the real estate brokerage business and your level of success and notoriety in the community through your previous marketing efforts will have a lot to do with how much marketing will need to take place in order for you to become a household name in your market. If you have already developed a good reputation in a particular neighborhood or community and you are going to expand your market share in that area, then you will need to create new marketing materials or enhance your existing marketing materials in order to build on your past and current successes. If, however, you are entering new territory, you will need to evaluate what marketing materials you have been using and ask yourself whether or not they will be effective in your new area.

You don't necessarily need to reinvent the wheel if your existing materials are high quality; just refine and enhance them to better reflect the new image that you and your team are all about. If your marketing materials up to this point were about you, then you will need to think through just how much you want to market your new team concept.

People today really seem to like the team approach to buying and selling real estate. Your new materials can talk about your enhanced ability to communicate with your clients and customers and how that benefits them because you or a team member are always available to them, or you can talk about the fact that you now have a highly specialized and always-available escrow administrator to better handle *"The whole concept of marketing is to create a brand name for yourself that consumers will equate with being well-cared for when they need real assistance."* every minute detail of their transaction and always be available to them when they have questions. Do you see the feature/benefit tie in here? That's what will get people's attention because it has meaning to them; they perceive that they will benefit from doing business with you, so be sure to put yourself in the customer's place and give the What's-In-It-For-Me (WIIFM) test to every piece of marketing and advertising material that you ever create.

The whole concept of marketing is to create a brand name for yourself that consumers will equate with being well-cared for when they need real assistance.

The niche market that you have chosen will certainly have a profound effect on the type of marketing pieces that you create. After you have decided on your niche market and created your marketing pieces, it is time to obtain a very up-to-date database of the customers whom you want to reach and begin a very sustained mailing program to them.

An introductory letter is the most effective way to start, but don't make the mistake of doing a mass mailing that will soon be forgotten. Instead, mail about 15 to 30 introductory letters a day and then follow up, or have your new assistant follow up 2 days later with a short telephone call asking if your letter was received. This allows for a dialogue between you and the customer or at least gives you the opportunity to leave a message so that the customer becomes familiar with your voice, and to a degree, your personality. It also increases the effectiveness of your mailing by as much as 15 percent with regard to the number of people who will remember you.

Your letter should be short. It should tell the target customer that you specialize somewhat in their neighborhood, or in selling their type of product (if the letter is to a builder, for example), and what the benefit of your services would be to them. It should also state that you will call them in a few days to see whether they got your letter and to see whether you can be of service to them.

After the initial letter and follow up, you should plan to mail something to them every 2 weeks to 8 weeks to quickly build name recognition; then you can mail monthly or as necessary and reasonable. Two of the most effective marketing pieces that you can mail to a target group like this are "Just Listed" (or "Just Sold") cards, as they tell the customer that you are active in that particular marketplace, and testimonial letters that you have received from current and past customers. These letters are especially powerful as they have an arms-length third-party credibility about them and are well read by curious consumers.

Upscale magazines, such as *Tucson Lifestyle Magazine*, are an expensive but excellent place to put marketing pieces that will help build your image to your newly targeted group. Again, be careful about your content and be sure that the ad conveys what the new you is all about, followed by a benefit to the reader for using your services.

In Chapter 12, you will read where Hugh Cornish, who sells more than 100 million dollars a year, creates and mails an annual business report on the state of the real estate industry in his local market. He brings in area, state, and national data as needed, uses graphs and quotes changes in appreciation rates, interest rates, and other things that have an effect on prices and marketing time in his market. People actually call him and ask for it. It is a highly effective marketing piece that gives him huge credibility.

> *"Above all, remember that consistency is the name of the game here, so after you start, don't stop."*

Above all, remember that consistency is the name of the game here, so after you start, don't stop.

Advertising

Advertising at the mega producer level is most often a multitiered issue. This is not about image building like marketing is, it is about getting people emotionally involved enough to contact you to see a specific property.

Newspaper advertising can be expensive, and, depending on where you live, you may only have one or two newspapers at your disposal. Nearly all of the agents that I have talked to tell me that they get more actual property inquiries from the smaller local papers than they do from the large metropolitan newspapers, although many of the larger papers, such as the *San Francisco Examiner/Chronicle* have zones that you can advertise in pretty effectively.

> *"When you advertise in the newspapers, remember to use the AIDA formula for maximum reader response."*

When you advertise in the newspapers, remember to use the AIDA formula for maximum reader response.

Attention: Readers scan ads; they don't read them all. Your ad needs to have a header or catchy word or phrase that will stand out and get readers to pause long enough to read the rest of your ad. Phrases like "Incredible view," "Shimmering pool," or "Nestled in the trees," are examples of short vision creating words that will entice the reader to go further.

Interest: After you have their attention, you need to immediately create interest in the next several words in order to get them to read the rest of the ad and not just skip it. Phrases that continue the first impression of the ad and build on it are very appropriate.

Desire: After you have gotten readers' attention and sustained their interest long enough to keep reading, you need to create desire. This is best accomplished by stating a major feature of the property followed by its benefit to the readers and should create a desire to get more information or to see the property. An example would be "Sparkling Pool. Summer is almost here, and your family and friends will love spending time cooling off in the large free-form pool offered in this beautifully maintained four-bedroom beauty."

Action (call to action): Now that you have a reader's full attention, you must ask him or her to take action on those feelings. The previous example finished off with "High-demand area and won't last long. Call Bob Herd today for a look at this great home!" This will get you many more calls and be a far better use of your advertising dollars than just citing facts about the house.

Target mailings are a highly effective method of advertising and should be an ongoing part of your business plan. This is accomplished by analyzing every listing that you get and asking yourself "who is the likely buyer for this property?" After you have identified who the likely buyer is, you can get address lists of people in these neighborhoods from your favorite title company and mail one of your property brochures directly to each of them with a short letter

> *"Target mailings are a highly effective method of advertising and should be an ongoing part of your business plan."*

or note telling them that you have listed the enclosed property and you thought that they might like to take a look at it; if they do, please give you a call for a private showing. I used this very effective method many, many times over the years and always had great luck with it.

You can also pull target buyers out of the Multiple Listing System (MLS) by searching by price or area for homes that are currently listed whose owners would be probable buyers for your listings. Be sure to keep it on a professional level and recommend that if they are interested in seeing your listing that they contact their agent and that you will be happy to work with them. You will find from time to time that someone will call you about your mailing, and they are very unhappy with their present agent because of poor service; they will be very pleased to meet with you as a buyer. Be sure to ask whether they have signed a Buyer/Broker Listing Agreement with their current agent. If they have, then you must not go any further with them.

Create a "Top 100" list. Get information from your Multiple Listing System about who the top 100 agents in your marketing area are and do a monthly mailing to them of your listings. This has two values. You will get showings of your homes by these highly effective agents, and more sales will result. You can also tell your sellers about this list, and if they want to overprice their property, tell them that you cannot include their property in this mailing. Explain that you must maintain a high degree of credibility to these busy agents in order for them to take the time to open your mail and review your listings. If you send them overpriced listings, your credibility will diminish, and it will hurt you and your other clients as well. It actually does help get better priced listings and price adjustments.

New home subdivision advertising is quite often a mix of advertising and marketing in the same ad. You are playing to a much broader consumer group than when you are selling an individual home, so you need to be very creative and very budget conscious.

"Don't be afraid to give your valuable input to them as well; just be sure to back up what you say with factual information."

If you are representing a custom home builder that buys a piece of land and builds several spec homes, you will advertise differently than if you were representing a major builder that is building a sizeable subdivision in stages. Their requirements are quite different, and you need to be keenly aware of what message they want to convey to the public. Interview each new home builder client at length to see what he or she feels is important to them. Don't be afraid to give your valuable input to them as well; just be sure to back up what you say with factual information.

I was recently asked to meet with a group of developers to review their preliminary plans for a new subdivision that they were planning for an excellent neighborhood in the Tucson market. In order to maximize land density, the builder was proposing a three-story townhome project with the garages at street level, and a two-story townhome above that. I asked him who he felt his target market was and he told me that it was the "snowbirds" who come here each winter to escape the harsh northeastern weather. I asked him whether he had considered their age, as the majority of them are in their late-50s to 80s, and they would not be inclined to want to handle multiple flights of stairs. He said, "Oh my, I was so caught up in land use density issues that I never thought of that." He was ready to scrap the whole concept when I suggested to him that due to the excellent location and the excellent school system in that area that the same project was still very viable with some minor changes such as adding a swimming pool, clubhouse, and playground that would appeal to younger families with school-aged children and teens and the very large college population. A different marketing and advertising approach would certainly be needed, but the demand was definitely there.

Company-Paid Advertising

Every real estate company has some sort of company-paid advertising that is shared on a fairly equal basis by all of the agents who work for the company. In your new role as a mega-producer, you will be bringing much more listing inventory into the company than the average sales agent. Advertising these properties is going to be a major part of your new operating budget. In order to minimize your financial outlay, you should have a meeting with your broker or branch manager and ask them to help you with this issue by seeing that you get your proportionate share of company-paid advertising. You will need to be aware that if you are on a very high commission split that the net financial benefit to the company may not be enough of an increase to warrant much more support, but it is certainly worth a discussion.

You will also need to assess how the company's advertising style and quality of advertising fits into your method of operation. If you are specializing in luxury home sales and your company or office uses the local black-and-white throwaway shopper for the majority of its advertising, then you have an image problem. The opposite may also apply where you specialize in a high-volume, lower priced homes that the local weekly newspaper is quite appropriate for and brings lots of calls, but where your company or office, which sells mostly upper-end homes, advertises only in the major regional newspaper because of the image that they want to maintain. If the company is not going to give you the additional company-paid advertising that your increased business warrants, then some type of allowance or reimbursement program is probably worth negotiating with them. This could be accomplished via company-paid newspaper advertising; just listed and just sold cards; an allowance for farming expenses, including postage and the creation of sales and marketing brochures at company expense. As the cost for all of the preceding comes right off of the company's bottom-line profits, which are very thin these days, don't expect the broker or manager to offer anything without some sort of prompting.

Using E-mail

E-mail is rapidly becoming one of the most effective types of group communication available today. Its uses are as boundless as your imagination. You can use it to keep clients and customers advised about the status of escrows that they are in; the progress of listings that you are marketing for them; new listings that you have taken that they, or someone that they know may be interested in; special interest items that you can pass along to a general group or to a group of your current and past clients that you have grouped together; target marketing of your listings to various groups that would have a high probability of being interested in them, and more. Just use your imagination!

"E-mail is rapidly becoming one of the most effective types of group communication available today."

I hired a wonderful lady here in Arizona as a new agent. As she began to sell, she would find out everything that she could about her clients and place them in both a general e-mail group and in any special group that dealt with their special interests, such as a love of dogs, or hobbies such as bicycling, gardening, etc. She is constantly on the watch for newsworthy items and when she finds them, she regularly e-mails them to her special interest groups. She also uploads pictures of her new listings and regularly e-mails them to all of her clients along with the general price and other basic information and asks whether anyone is interested in seeing it.

Her sellers love it as a very effective way of marketing their home; her clients all think that she is a marketing genius; and she sells a number of her own listings. She also never fails to remind her e-mail recipients that she works strictly by referral and really appreciates their referrals. She was my Rookie of the Year her first year in real estate and will exceed eight million dollars in sales her third year. She is well on her way to becoming a mega-producer by year five.

One thing that you must be very careful about and sensitive to is that most people don't want their e-mail addresses shared with other people without their permission. You could lose clients quickly this way. To avoid this, when you are making mass or grouped e-mails to people, send the e-mail to yourself and "BCC" or blind copy the group. They will all come to *"Most people don't want their e-mail addresses shared with other people without their permission."* know that e-mail that they receive with your name on it is worth opening up, and they will all appreciate the anonymity.

Do not forward spam e-mails such as jokes and chain letters to your clients. People's tastes are too divergent for that sort of thing to appeal to your whole group; you will soon lose credibility; and your e-mails will be deleted without even being opened. It is very important that you keep your e-mails on a very professional level.

5

Building Your Team

*E*ach of you will have different aspirations as to where you want to take your businesses. Many of you will hire only one licensed assistant and maybe a buyer's representative, grow your business to 15 or 20 million dollars a year on a sustained basis, and be quite happy with that. A lot of you will hire two, three, or more licensed assistants, maybe ten or more buyer's representatives, and two or three telemarketers and grow your business exponentially for many, many years to come, probably to more than 100 million dollars in annual sales. In either case, if you intelligently and progressively add staff to your team as needed, you will create a viable business that will have inherent value and create an asset that you can sell for a large sum of money and several years of referral fees later in your career.

You each have one thing in common; you want far more than you are now getting out of the real estate brokerage business. You could just work harder and work more hours, but that is guaranteed to burn you out and is not the truly professional way to grow your business on a sustained basis and give incredible service at the same time. The only way to achieve your goal is to create a business plan that gives you both leverage and a working blueprint of what you need to do in timely, controlled phases to create the demand for your services and add the staff to your team to handle it at the same time.

> *"You each have one thing in common; you want far more than you are now getting out of the real estate brokerage business."*

Let's take a look at the job descriptions of each of your potential team members and talk a little about their key roles and why they are so important to your team.

The Office Manager or Escrow Administrator

The office manager position is really a general title for the first person that you hire. He or she should be licensed in the state that you are working, as that person will be communicating with your clients on a regular basis, many times even giving your clients suggestions about how to respond to requests for property repairs, what certain things on a title report mean, and other things of that nature. It is far too easy for an office manager to cross the line and provide real estate services without a license than good business practices would dictate, so I strongly urge you to have every person who works on your team become licensed. There is also a credibility and knowledge issue that this person will bring to the table by being licensed.

From personal experience, I can tell you that the Real Estate Professional Assistant (REPA) course that is given by the National Association of REALTORS® is well worth having any and all of your new assistants attend. I sent my office Administrator and my escrow administrator through this course at my own expense, and it has repaid me over and over due to their heightened awareness of the sales/escrow process and what the agent actually goes through during that process. I suggest that you, too, would reap great rewards from using it. It is a 2-day course that is taught at the real estate training schools or is sponsored by the local real estate association education committees. The Women's Council of REALTORS also sponsors these types of educational classes as well.

In the beginning, and sometimes on a permanent basis, your office manager will also be your escrow administrator. He or she will need to be thoroughly trained on escrow procedures in your area. Some of you use closing attorneys in your area, and others use escrow officers, so your duties and those of your administrator will vary by area.

Your administrator should know how to open an escrow; provide all necessary data about the property and your client or customer to the escrow officer or closing attorney; see that any earnest money deposit checks are properly logged and placed with the proper parties in the time allotted by your state regulations (usually the company trust account or the escrow company); ask you what inspections your client wants, order them for you, and then inform you of the dates and times; and communicate all of this information to the co-op agent, if there is one. As title reports, inspections, appraisals, repair requests, and other pertinent documents are received, they should be trained on how to read them and look for "red flag" or problematic items and areas and inform you of them. At your direction, these disclosures, reports, and other documents should be sent out to the co-op agent and/or your clients for review and signatures. One of their most important duties is the timely dissemination of information and seeing that proper signatures are obtained for your file copies. They will need to be extremely aware of important dates, such as escrow closing dates, contingency waiver dates, moving dates, and so on, and keep you well informed of them in advance. Your office manager should also keep a very accurate record of your current and past clients. This should include their names and home addresses; the address and description of any rental property owned; the names of their children; birthdays; anniversaries, if you know them; all telephone numbers, any pets and/or hobbies; and any other information that you deem important.

> *"One of their most important duties is the timely dissemination of information and seeing that proper signatures are obtained for your file copies.*
>
> *Your office manager should also keep a very accurate record of your current and past clients."*

Your office manager may do several off-site duties *of assistant* at first, but those duties probably will best be delegated to the first licensed assistant that you hire. These duties include stocking the flyer bins at your listings; replacing sign-in sheets at the property; calling the agents that showed the property for customer feedback; taking time-sensitive paperwork and documents to other agents, lenders, clients, escrow officers, and appraisers; and installing or removing keyboxes, just to mention a few.

Assistant

Your office manager is literally an extension of you to the rest of the world, and you need to be extremely careful about whom you hire. They will not only need to be computer literate and technically savvy, they absolutely must have top communication and people skills. At this writing, this position seems to demand from $10 an hour for a new and relatively inexperienced person, to $20 an hour plus some type of bonus for a highly experienced person with several years experience as an agent. One highly experienced assistant that I know with almost 30 years of experience as an agent gets $20 an hour and a $500 bonus for every million dollars in sales volume that the agent closes each month. I also know of some office managers who receive a straight 10 percent of each commission check paid to the agent. This, of course, works when you have only one assistant.

Depending on where your financial reserves are, where you are headed, and how fast you intend to get there, you may want to hire a part-time assistant at first and then grow into two or more part-time assistants or have the part-time assistant become full time. What you do not want to do is share an assistant with another agent. As one or both of you grow your business to the point of needing a full-time assistant, you are heading for an argument about who gets the existing one, and the relationship will certainly suffer.

> *"What you do not want to do is share an assistant with another agent."*

Current real estate agents are an excellent source of team members. Many find that they do not like the weekend work or odd hours, and a number of people who come into the real estate business have incredibly good people and organizational skills but just don't have that "thing" that makes them work well in our unstructured environment. All of these people should be investigated for your administrative needs, and they are already licensed and have a good sense of what you go through in the operation of your business.

The Licensed Assistant

As I stated previously, all of your team members should be licensed. Depending on the size of your organization, you may or may not find several of these job descriptions overlapping. The licensed assistant actually can play many roles. I have seen several instances in which a licensed assistant does all of the escrow work and acts as a buyer's representative on an as-needed basis. This can work fairly well when you are first starting to build your team. I have also seen the opposite, in which a person hired primarily as a buyer's representative will be delegated some escrow work from time to time. I have seen agents hired as a combination telemarketer and buyer's representative. I think that

> *"The licensed assistant actually can play many roles."*

the important message here is to assess the strengths of your team members and put them to work where they have the most passion for the role that they play.

The term "licensed assistant is almost redundant as everyone on your team should be licensed; however, this title usually is reserved for your team members who will be acting in a direct front-line capacity with your clients; that is, either showing them property as a buyer's representative, telemarketing to get you listing appointments, or communicating with them regularly through the course of an escrow.

The pay scale for a licensed assistant is as divergent as the job description itself and will need careful assessment on your part prior to the actual employment interview. If you are going to have a licensed assistant who will perform any combination of the tasks related in this chapter, then you will need to clearly define the total job first and then see what method or combination of methods makes sense for that job. Do not wait until you are conducting the interview with someone whom you really want to hire to start thinking about how you are going to compensate them, because if you are not reasonable you will scare them away, and if you act too quickly, you could give away the store, so to speak. Be reasonable, put on the hat of the person that you are going to hire, ask yourself what makes sense in the way of compensation for having that job done to the degree of excellence that you will require, and then be willing to pay it to the right person.

The Buyer's Representative

This person's job is to receive buyer referrals from you , to generate buyers by their own efforts, and to sell them homes on your behalf. The best buyer's representative is probably the agent who is good at selling homes to people, but not so good at getting people to sell to. They need you and your supply of buyers more than you need their efforts. The agent that is good at generating their own buyer leads is far more likely to leave you and go on their own after a time than one that relies heavily on you as a source of their business. Overall, the sense of personal fulfillment

"Overall, the sense of personal fulfillment that a person gets from belonging to your team will be the dominant factor with regards to their longevity with you."

that a person gets from belonging to your team will be the dominant factor with regards to their longevity with you.

Do your own assessment of the agents in your local area and ask your branch manager about agents whom he or she knows who would be good candidates. It is important that this person obtains the Accredited Buyer's Representative (ABR) designation, which is offered through the National Association of REALTORS®. It is a short 2-day course that is usually offered through your local association or license training school. This intense course really emphasizes their role as the buyer's representative and teaches them how to effectively work with all types of buyers while maintaining a high professional standard, both for you and the industry. Given the fact that the overwhelming majority of litigation against real estate professionals comes from buyers, this course is really worth its weight in gold.

It is critical that you either have a close, even intimate knowledge of how a potential addition to your buyer's representative team works, or that you are able to investigate the candidate thoroughly. Don't be in a huge rush here; this person is essentially going to "be you" to the buyers that you send him or her, so investigate them thoroughly. Ask for references from agents whom they have worked with in the past and, if applicable, for buyers that they have represented in the past.

> *"Ask for references from agents whom they have worked with in the past and, if applicable, for buyers that they have represented in the past."*

You will need to either create your own referral form or use the one that I have supplied at the end of this chapter each time that you assign a buyer to one of your reps. This is mainly for accountability purposes. Each time that you give a buyer to a representative of yours, it is a potential commission check for both of you. You will want a weekly status report on every referral that you have made from the time that you make it through the time that escrow closes and you are notified that they are logged into your database as a past client. See Chapter 9 for further details about status meetings.

Compensation for a buyer's representative can also vary widely and is dictated by what experience and skills they bring to the table and how

many buyers you will refer to them. I know one agent who takes a 30 percent referral fee from the first closing with a referred buyer, a 25 percent referral fee from the next two transactions with that referral, and then nothing after that. Any listings that are generated from that referral are the property of the business owner who referred the listing. I also know of agents who take a 25 percent referral fee on the first referral each month, 35 percent for the second one, and 50 percent for

---

Office Manager/Escrow Administrator

1. Tell me about the best job that you've ever had and what you liked the most about it.

2. Tell me about the worst job and what you disliked about it the most.

3. What type of experience do you have in conducting all of the issues involved in an escrow?

4. Have you had to direct the activities of other people before? Please explain or elaborate.

5. Are you aware of what the responsibilities of this position are? (Be prepared to explain them.)

6. Are you currently licensed in this state?

7. In the beginning, if you are selected, you may be required to input listings into the MLS, create flyers and distribute them to the owners' homes, and things of that nature, until we build the team. How do you think that you could handle that?

8. If you are tentatively selected, we will need references from two past employers, and, if you acted as an agent in the past, we will need references from two past clients. Will you provide these?

9. Tell me a little about why you are changing careers at this time.

10. What questions do you have for me at this time?

any subsequent ones. The logic there is that if a buyer's representative is handed three or more sales a month, he or she should be willing to share generously in the pie.

This is probably a good time to mention that all team members who work for you should have a written contract with you that clearly spells out, at a minimum, their duties, compensation, independent

---

Licensed Assistant Interview Sheet

1. How long have you been licensed in this state?

2. Are you licensed in any other state? Any plans to go back there?

3. Tell me about your real estate career if you've had one and what prompted you to sell real estate.

4. What prompts you to make the transition from sales into the licensed assistant position?

5. What was the best job that you've ever had, and what did you like the most about it.

6. What former job did you like the least, and why?

7. Are you aware of the many duties that are required of a licensed assistant? (Be prepared to explain the various tasks that may be assigned.)

8. If you are tentatively selected, you will need to supply us with at least two former clients and two agents as references. Will you be able to do that?

9. What questions do you have for me at this time?

contractor or employee status, the fact that it is an "at will" contract, and any other issues that you and your attorney decide are important. You can create a rough draft agreement well in advance of hiring someone, but have it reviewed by an attorney before you use it; or better yet, see whether some other mega-agent has already visited that issue and would be willing to share their agreements with you for a small fee.

Buyers Representative Interview Sheet

Ask for and read the applicant's resume first.

1. Tell me about the best job that you've ever had, and what you liked the most about it.

2. Tell me about the worst job you've had, and what you didn't like about it the most.

3. Can you work well with minimal direction?

4. Have you heard of the (your team name) before?

5. Do you know how our sales team functions and what your role would be if you were hired? (Explain if necessary, including the pay schedule and ask how they feel about it.)

6. How do you feel about working weekends and some holidays?

7. Are you currently licensed in this state or any others?

8. How will you deal with working on primarily a commission income?

9. What benefit do you see in working as a buyer's representative with our team versus what you are doing now?

10. If you are tentatively selected, we will need at least two agent references and two past customer references who we can contact. Can you supply us with those if we ask?

11. What questions about the position do you have for me right now?

The Telemarketer

This person's entire job is lead generation. His or her job is to keep you busy making listing presentations. Many mega-agents do not use a telemarketer. When I asked them why, few could really give me a definitive answer why they don't, except for a perception that they didn't need one to remain as busy as they want to be from the other sources of listings that are available to them. Your tenure as a real estate profes-

---

Telemarketer Interview Sheet

Ask for and review the applicant's resume first

1. Tell me about any positions that you've had that required telemarketing skills.

2. What was the best job that you've ever had, and what did you like the most about it?

3. What was your worst job, and what did you like the least about it?

4. What are your thoughts about people who are rude to you over the telephone?

5. Tell me a little about your past work as a real estate licensee.

6. If you worked as a real estate agent, did you cold call on your own behalf? Where and how often?

7. Have you ever worked on a performance-based salary and bonus system before? How do you feel about that?

8. If you are tentatively selected, you will be required to give us at least two past clients and two previous employers as references. Will you be able to do that?

9. What questions do you have for me at this time?

sional will have a lot to do with your decision to use a telemarketer or not. If you have a large number of listings continually coming to you from referral and repeat clients, an on-going mailing campaign like David Vanneste has, a successful on-going For Sale By Owner program, or other sources of listings, then this is simply a decision that you will have to make. I did observe a perception by the agents that I interviewed who sell high-end properties that they thought that their target audience would not identify well with being contacted by a telemarketer. I'm not sure that this perception is completely accurate as it seems that it hasn't really been tested for any reasonable duration of time and done by a person who has been trained with this very issue in mind.

> *"This person's entire job is lead generation."*

An agent in Arizona who worked for me told me that when he divided the annual income that he made that could be attributed directly to telemarketing by the number of hours that he spent telemarketing, he made more than $4,000.00 per hour. He works mainly in the lower-mid and mid-price range.

It is very important that your telemarketer is highly trained by you so that every call that he or she makes on your behalf is a credit to you and your organization. Either you, or someone whose judgment you trust implicitly, needs to thoroughly train this person to the point that they are the consummate professional at what they do. This is best done by first developing a short, easy-approach script and then role playing it until it is perfection before they ever make that first call. It doesn't really take long; I have done it many times with agents who have worked for me over the years. You can refer back to Chapter 3 for an example of a script that is nonoffensive and produces listing leads.

Accountability will again come in to play here as well as having a properly written method of transmitting listing leads to you. You will need to have a form that the telemarketer uses to write down the number of calls made, to whom they were made, the date and time that they were made, and the results. This information should be retained by you and your telemarketer and analyzed periodically. You need to analyze it to see whether your telemarketer is getting more personal contacts (instead of answering machines) at a given time of day or on one day versus another. After they have done this for you for several months, an analysis of this type of information will help to increase their effectiveness. Your telemarketer(s) will also need to keep records of where they have called so that they do not call in any given area too often. New federal laws that regulate unsolicited calls, and both you and your telemarketer need to be aware of and carefully follow these rules. Your local real estate association should be able to provide you with any restrictions.

When someone shows interest and an appointment is made, you need to be notified in writing. There should be a form for this as well. Your telemarketer should have a current copy of your scheduled appointments so that he or she can schedule a listing appointment for you and quickly notify you without getting you double-scheduled.

Compensation for telemarketers varies as well. I know several agents that pay their telemarketer a base salary of $1,500.00 per month plus a bonus of $750.00 to $1,500.00 for each escrow closed monthly that was generated by the telemarketer's efforts. A few agents that I know pay a straight 10–15 percent referral fee for each telemarketer-generated escrow that closes. A good telemarketer who gets several appointments per month can make an excellent living with this type of compensation. This can be tough, tedious work at times, and the rewards need to be very enticing to keep a good telemarketer, so interview carefully, hire the very best, and pay them very well. You and the rest of your team will prosper greatly for it.

Part-Time Help

The use of part-time help will be very efficient for you financially. It will help you to get many tasks done efficiently as well as for minimal cost. You will need someone to do computer work for you such as updating your client list, creating labels for mail outs, filling *"The use of part-time help will be very efficient for you financially."* flyer bins, creating brochures for your new listings, taking digital pictures of your new listings, and so on, which will absolutely not require a real estate license. These tasks are very necessary and important to the success of your team and your business, but they can be done, and done well, by mature college students, stay-at-home-moms who want a little income, and others who bring a maturity and pride in their work to their job, but either don't want, or can't do a full-time job.

Here in Arizona, this is $6.00–$9.00 an hour work. You absolutely should not be doing these tasks as your hourly rate is far higher than that. This position is strictly an hourly wage type of job, with accountability on their part to do the work properly and timely. Your office administrator should be empowered to oversee the work of any part-time people who are hired to do work for your team.

Other Agents in Your Company

Your new team is going to generate many, many new listings. Although we, as real estate professionals, know that open houses are not really very efficient at getting the property sold, many sellers are very demanding about including them in your marketing plan.

To handle this, you have several options. You can assign them to your buyer's representatives and/or to your licensed assistants on a minimum per month basis, but this may well put them in conflict with their primary responsibilities of working with your referral buyers or other proactive business generating activities. A buyer's representative should never be made to hold an open house; they should be out with buyers at every opportunity. A licensed assistant who is not specifically designated as only a buyer's representative probably can be called on once or twice a month to assist you in holding your homes open.

> *"A buyer's representative should never be made to hold an open house; they should be out with buyers at every opportunity."*

One of the major advantages in working for a major company with a lot of agents is that there are always an abundance of new and newer agents who both need and want to hold an open house on a regular basis. It is very wise of you to take advantage of this as it takes the pressure off of you, there is no charge for their services, and a perceived need of the seller is met. Obviously, whoever it is on your team that handles scheduling open houses (again, not you) will have to carefully screen each agent for quality. The last thing that you want is an agent who is unreliable and just doesn't show up (oh, does that make the sellers angry!), or shows up but has an unprofessional manner. Remember, your reputation is only as good as the people who work for you.

over load

From time to time, you may reach a point in the growth of your organization where you are simply overwhelmed with too many listings or too many buyers. This is a nice problem to have, but it is a problem and can be overwhelming at times. This usually happens when the

"From time to time, you may reach a point in the growth of your organization where you are simply overwhelmed with too many listings or too many buyers."

people whom you have hired have fully matured into their roles as a part of your team and are in full swing generating new business.

Instead of making the mistake of quickly hiring a new buyer's representative or licensed assistant and letting your standard go down because of the current need, consider either co-listing a property with one of the better new agents in your office if you're overloaded with listings, or refer a buyer to a good newer agent for a referral fee. This is a temporary situation only and will end quickly as you hire additional staff to fill the void. It gets the job done well; you have a happy buyer or seller; and, just maybe, if the agent performed well, you have a new team member.

Freeloader Agents

As a manager for more than 30 years, I have witnessed many, many occasions in which a mega-agent is approached by an agent in the same office or same company who wants to get on the team. They usually have a track record of poor performance, poor people skills, laziness, or other maladies that make them inferior agents. They will approach you, often in a rather bold fashion, and tell you in some way that you simply can't exist without them, and they will suggest that you would be very smart to co-list one of your listings with them or that you should refer a buyer to them. It can be just short of confrontational at times and put you on the spot in an embarrassing way. Unfortunately, almost all of you will have this happen to you. If you do, the best way to handle the situation is to simply tell them that you have everything handled very well at the moment and that you will not be adding to your staff anytime soon. If they persist, and some will, and ask if you will hire them later, state that you have very high standards for your team members and when you are ready to hire someone they can submit a resume, and you will look it over before you make a selection. After they have been passed over a few times, they usually get the picture and quit pestering you. If someone gets obnoxious or even confrontational with you, and, yes, I have actually seen this happen, that's the time to say that they don't measure up to the standards that you have set for your team members. They will get upset and won't talk to you after that in all likelihood, and isn't that a shame! The other people in your office will quietly admire you for what you have done. Again, I am speaking from actual experience, both personally and as a manager.

Additional Staff

The issue of adding staff is always a balancing act between a perceived need and the financial ability to finance the new team member through their transition period. *"You should make a cash reserve account a part of your operating budget."* That's why you should make a cash reserve account a part of your operating budget.

One only has to look at the methods of compensation described earlier in this chapter to see that you may have an outlay of several thousand dollars before a new team member starts to become a profit center. This is normal in every business. Every real estate branch manager makes this decision every time he or she hires a new or fairly new, but untrained agent.

Depending on how close you are with your office manager/escrow administrator, it will be wise on your part to have a meeting with him or her and assess the current needs of the team. Quite often, they are more attuned to the personnel needs than you are; it's their job. The strength of the real estate market at any given time should also be assessed when making these types of decisions.

If the market is robust or stable and you think that it will remain so and your buyer's representatives are showing signs that they are overloaded, then you may really have a need to add another one, however, if sales are declining, the average days on the market is going up, interest rates are increasing and the news is reporting that consumer confidence is eroding and unemployment is increasing, then you make the opposite decision and stay lean for at least the short term.

To maximize your team's growth and opportunities, you need to stay very aware of the rise and fall of the market and be ready to quickly

up and down market

jump on what look like sustained upturns in the market. This can really increase your market share and your bottom-line profit.

Depending on what niche market you work and what path your regular activities have gotten you into, you probably will have the opportunity to take on a new subdivision or a new condominium project. If you do this right, it can lead to a whole new on-going source of income for you; however, there is a lot of very specialized knowledge needed to take on projects like these. You may need to give advice on everything from what the highest and best use of a particular tract of land is, to what type of architectural style is proper for a particular market, or you may be asked to present a full-blown marketing and advertising campaign.

> *"To maximize your team's growth and opportunities, you need to stay very aware of the rise and fall of the market and be ready to quickly jump on what look like sustained upturns in the market."*

If you are already skilled at these types of things, like Nikki Mehalic is, then you are way ahead of the game, but if you are unfamiliar with this type of client representation, then get someone who is to do the project with you. Remember, your reputation as a true professional, as well as the client's best interests are both best served by having someone with a complete understanding of the project and what it will take to make it a success.

As a mega-producer, you will develop a high degree of skill in a certain area of real estate, and you will likely be called on from time to time to co-list a project of this type, or whatever your specialty is, by a newer agent, so think with an *abundance mentality* about new ventures that are offered to you and whether you need to bring in another knowledgeable person or team. Then do so knowing that at a later date you will be on the receiving end of such a request because of your greater knowledge.

Other Team Members

If you do any subdivision work, you will need to hire site agents to be at the project every day to greet visitors and to write contracts on your behalf.

Site Agents

The site agent is perceived as a lucrative position by many real estate agents, and you must be very careful in your hiring process. Picking the right people who are highly motivated and very responsible will ensure the success of your role in the venture and surely get you future business from that developer, but if you pick the wrong people, things can get off to a bad start, and then get worse from there.

Try to get referrals of licensed agents who already have a good track record with one or more previous site sale positions. A good second choice is agents who are known to be effective at holding an open house and getting names and phone numbers and then following up with the customers and making sales happen with them.

You are certain to be approached by marginal agents who are looking for what they perceive as an easy way to make a sale. Do not hire these people. If asked about a position, tell them that you don't need any-one at this time or tell them to submit a resume to you, and you will pass it along to the developer for review, and then dump it in the trash can. These are the people who will show up for work late or not at all, offend potential buyers by their lack of product knowledge and poor people skills, and generally wreak havoc on your project.

Advertising and Marketing Coordinator

Your new team will start to produce a large number of listings. The owners of these properties will have expectations of seeing their home marketed and advertised in various ways. This person's job is to see that each property receives the attention that is required to do a good job and keep both you and the owners happy.

Many factors, such as price, type of property, location, and market conditions, will dictate just what types of marketing and advertising you do for each listing that you have, which may include such things as placement into the Multiple Listing Service (MLS), newspaper ads, virtual home tours that are made available on your company's or your Web site, and the creation of marketing and sales brochures. This person should also be primarily responsible for

"Be very careful about your selection of this person as he or she will have a profound effect on your team's and your reputation."

Hold 2 - 5 open houses in the same area [handwritten]

placing all of your open house ads and securing agents to hold all of them open. Be very careful about your selection of this person as he or she will have a profound effect on your team's and your reputation. Owners simply expect the job to be done flawlessly, and a missed open house, in which the owners are waiting expectantly for an agent to show up and who never does can wreak havoc on you and give you a reputation as someone who isn't organized.

The pay rate for this person can vary widely, and the position is often filled by one of your licensed assistants. This position usually can be effectively filled on a part-time basis by one of your licensed assistants; however, if your licensed assistants are all pretty much working at full capacity, then consider hiring a part-time person for this position, which should pay around $9.00 to $11.00 an hour, depending on where you live.

There are two good sources for this type of person. The first is an agent whom you know who has a reputation for writing creative ads and has demonstrated good attention to detail and deadlines. The second, and probably the best source, is to contact the account representative that you always use at your local newspaper and ask him or her whether they know of anyone that is working at, or used to work in the paper's advertising department who may be looking for a part-time job. A person like that, who is currently or used to help real estate agents place ads will be very well versed on writing effective ads and working under deadlines.

Being the Boss

You are about to make a significant shift in your own job description. As a real estate agent, you were your own boss, and you worked as effectively as you could while being responsible only to yourself and the broker or manager of your company. Now you are going to have to become the boss, assuming responsibility for the direction of independent contractors and employees. It works two ways; you will be responsible for seeing that they perform at peak efficiency for your team in order to promote growth, meet net profit expectations, and maintain your reputation. You will also be responsible for generating enough revenue into your team to meet its operating expenses, including the salaries that they will come to rely upon.

This is not a time to hire friends unless you know in advance that they absolutely sparkle at the task for which you are hiring them. If they perform poorly, you either have to put up with their inadequacy or run the risk of losing a friend. Remember, this is a business—a serious business—and you need to run it like one.

You will need to foster a sense of family within your team to create a harmonious working environment and promote longevity and loyalty, but you will also need to maintain your position as the boss. You are sure to be challenged by the "I'm an independent contractor, you can't tell me what to do" syndrome at some point, and you will need to be prepared to deal with it. If you hire someone to be the operational manager in your place, it is of paramount importance that you give him or her clear responsibility and authority to act on your behalf with the other people on your team and back them up when they must exercise that authority with any or all of the team members. I know first hand what it is like to be hired into that position and make some very necessary but unpopular new requirements of the team members to make them accountable to the business owner, only to have them go around me to the owner, and have the owner rescind the changes that I made to keep things harmonious. It was an awful experience, and, of course, I left the position as soon as possible.

Being the boss means, above all else, a leadership role for you. Your team will mirror what happens in every real estate office or company, where the office takes on the energy, enthusiasm, and personality of the manager or broker/owner. Your team will constantly be looking to you for leadership and guidance. If you have carefully hired the right people, they will very much want to be just like you, and whether you are aware of it or not, you will be on stage at all times, especially in times of crisis. Remember, your main job as the owner of the business is that of "Rainmaker," or business-generator, but it is also you, as the *boss*, who must take the leadership role necessary to ensure that your team runs smoothly and efficiently for the sake of the entire team. You do not need to be liked, but you must be respected.

> *"Being the boss means, above all else, a leadership role for you."*

REFERRAL AGREEMENT

Date_____

This is a: Listing____ Buyer____ Co-listing ____ referral that is being given to *(agent's name)*, hereinafter called "referred agent" by *(your name)*.

The above-named agent agrees to accept the referral or co-listing and agrees to provide full service to the client through escrow closing, to include any after-escrow issues, and further agrees to pay *(your name)* a referral fee as follows:

1. On each buyer or listing referral, the agent agrees to pay *(your name)* a referral fee of 30 percent of the commission received for the referred side of the transaction.

2. *(your name)* shall also receive a referral fee of 25 percent of any commissions earned by the "referred agent" from listing or selling activities with the referred client for the next three transactions done with the client after this transaction.

3. If this is a co-listing, then *(your name)* shall receive _____ percent of the listing commission, and the "referred agent" shall receive _____ percent of the listing commission. If the "referred agent" represents the buyer in the transaction, a referral fee shall be due to *(your name)* pursuant to paragraphs 1 and 2 above.

_____   _____
(your name)   Referred agent

    Date _____   Date _____

Client name_____

Address _____

Work number _____ Home number _____

Email_____

Comments _____

_____

_____

_____

6

Support from Your Company

Office Space

We need to put this issue into the proper perspective. Mega-producers tend to be on extremely high commission splits, many with negotiated ceilings on the income that the company will retain from their earnings. This means that after giving you a certain number of desks or space, they start to lose money because they have to pay for additional space for you from which they obtain no revenue.

To every broker/owner or branch manager, each desk represents a profit center. Each desk or desk space that he or she gives to an agent to support a growing team means that the team must become effective enough to reasonably maintain the profit level of that desk, or the office starts to lose potential income. This is offset to a degree by the large volume of business that you do as a mega-producer and the enhanced positive exposure that your team's listing and sales activities give to the office or company.

"To every broker/ owner or branch manager, each desk represents a profit center."

For instance, if you allow agents in the office to hold your listings open, particularly new and newer agents, it helps them to meet clients and become productive faster, which makes the office more money, so this can be somewhat of an offset to the reduced potential revenue issue.

Depending on just how large of a team you create, you may be faced with taking on some office space of your own. This can be costly, and you probably will be asked to sign a lease for as many as one to five years or more, so be very careful about your expansion plans when you get to this point.

If the real estate company or branch office that you work for has unused space available (i.e., empty desks or unused space) and you have grown to the point where you need more space, ask the broker or manager if you can rent the available space at a reduced rate. As long as you bring enhanced revenue into the office to offset the extra space that they give to you, they should be fairly open to some type of arrangement. If they are not, and you are at a point where you must obtain more space, then you are at a major decision-making crossroad in your business expansion.

If you really like the company that you are with and wouldn't think of changing, then you will have to either obtain space of your own, as Nikki Mehalic and David Vanneste have done, or think about moving to another firm or opening your own firm. Neither of these options are something that you should consider unless you just absolutely have to as they are always disruptive to your business and expensive to do. See "Should You Open Your Own Firm" later in this chapter for an in-depth discussion of this highly important issue.

home office

Depending on the scale of your operation and what type of home you own, you may be able to have some of your staff work from your home. Many homes have an in-law unit, rental unit, or a garage that has been converted into a playroom or den. These separate quarters can make for very inexpensive and highly effective home offices that you and/or your team members who do not interface with the public can use quite effectively. If possible, you might even want to think about adding on to your home in some manner that would create this environment for you and your team rather than leasing office space.

Forms and Supplies

It is established tradition that each real estate company provides the forms that are necessary to use in the normal conduct of a real estate transaction; the only exceptions being the 100-percent companies, which require the agents to purchase their own for obvious reasons. Each company seems to have its own set of internal forms that it uses to track listings and escrows and to see that all state and federally-mandated forms are in the file as required. These should also be available to you at no charge. You will begin to use forms that you create within your team with which to interview and hire team members, refer clients to team members, and track the effectiveness of each team member and the team as a whole. It is not the company's responsibility to maintain your internal forms for you, and you should make provisions to create and store your internal forms within your own space.

Throughout this book are forms created for you to use. Please feel free to change them to fit your particular type of operation or style. The important thing is to have forms created and available to keep track of every important operational aspect of your business.

Administrative Assistance

As your business grows, you will find that you have an ever-growing need for additional administrative assistance. Not just paper shuffling, but proper handling of telephone calls, sending and receiving paperwork from other brokers and agents, assigning and receiving referrals, and a myriad of other tasks. Your office or company obviously will provide much of this support, depending on its size, but they are sure to limit it to the normal, general tasks that the office's administrative staff does for every agent.

As a mega-producer, you bring much in the way of business enhancement to the firm. Just how much extra help you are entitled to in return for what you produce can be a source of some very serious debate; for instance, the company that I am with provides partial reimbursement for a licensed assistant after an agent has reached a certain level of per-

> *"As a mega-producer, you bring much in the way of business enhancement to the firm."*

formance. If you are negotiating any administrative support issues with your company, this can be an excellent place to create something sensible for both of you.

If you are working at a smaller company that does not have the multi-tiered support staff usually found at the larger companies and if you are going to be producing business at the level that we are talking about here, then you will need to have a serious talk with your broker to see just what type of support he or she is willing to add on in order to handle all of it. Depending on commission split issues and other perks, it probably isn't fair for the company to reap such a huge reward and give you no more in the way of support than the average agent that brings in far less net profit to them than you do.

If your company employs any part-time help and you like the quality of the work that one or more of these people provide, get your manager's or broker's approval first, and then talk to these people about taking another part-time position with your team. They are already familiar with how the company works and are usually easier to train within your group. They could work a full eight-hour day with the company paying for half, and you paying for the other half. There are potential conflict-of-interest and privacy issues that arise here, so you will need to address them very carefully with the broker and the assistant that you are considering before you hire anyone like this.

Should You Open Your Own Firm?

As a new mega-producer, the answer is probably somewhere between probably not and an emphatic no! Remember where your strength lies; it's not in being an administrative manager, it's in being a rainmaker or business generator, and if you open your own firm you *will* need to give up a huge amount of time to the proper administration of the office. As it is, you'll be distracted enough by the members of your team, although if you get the right office manager to handle your team and give him or her full authority to act on your behalf, you will find the intrusions on your time to be minimal.

In Chapter 12, you will read conversations with four time-tested mega-producers and virtually all of them want nothing to do with owning and operating a real estate company and losing all of that valuable time to administrative duties; you probably shouldn't either.

About the only exception that I can think of would be if you are currently working at an office or company that just doesn't, or isn't capable of supporting your new expanded business model, and there isn't a firm in the same general marketing area that does. This may leave you with little or no choice but to open and run your own real estate company. In this case, I recommend that you purchase a copy of my first book, *Real Estate Office Management: A Guide To Success*, and read it thoroughly more than once before making any lasting decisions.

During the course of my 31-year career in the real estate brokerage business, I have seen that, overwhelmingly, the agents that become an icon by starting at and staying at one office are the highest paid individuals with the highest rate of repeat and referral business generated in the industry. So my advice is to think twice before you make a move, and only do it as a last resort and not merely for ego gratification.

Partnerships

Read again if a Partnership is entered into

It's a Marriage, Like It or Not

In my book on real estate office management, I talk about partnerships and how fragile the overwhelming majority of them are. The mega-producer who decides to form a partnership with one or more other agents is subject to the same issues that the partners of a newly formed real estate brokerage firm are—maybe even more. I have seen many partnerships created by average real estate agents over the years, almost all of which have failed after a time, but I have never seen a partnership at the mega-producer level that lasted more than a few weeks. I am sure that there are some highly effective exceptions, but they are rare indeed.

A partnership of this sort is the equivalent of a marriage in nearly every way. You will become deeply involved with and subject to the differences in personality of at least one other person who feels that he or she has just as much right to run things as you do. Maybe they do, and maybe they don't, but if they are your partner, they will certainly think that they do, and this can and usually does bring about tension in the workplace.

> *"A partnership of this sort is the equivalent of a marriage in nearly every way."*

Real estate agents, especially top performers like you, tend to be very independent by nature; that's what got them to where they are today. When they find themselves married to a new partner who has what can often be vastly different opinions about how things should be run, what direction to take the business, what areas to specialize in, and who to hire, things can get tense really quickly, and your energy and enthusiasm for the new venture can be sapped just as quickly . I am highly opinionated about this issue: Do not get involved in any form of partnership with another agent except for your spouse, and think that over carefully!

Should You, or Shouldn't You?

Far too many partnerships are created out of a perceived financial need rather than a well-thought out plan of action. What happens is that a rising star agent has everything that it takes to be a huge success by building a team to leverage his or her skills and become a major player in a certain market area; however, he or she doesn't go through the planning stage first to see whether it is feasible for them to do so, both from a business and a financial standpoint. Instead they sort of crunch some numbers and decide that it's too risky for them to be hiring people and

> *"Far too many partnerships are created out of a perceived financial need rather than a well-thought out plan of action."*

taking on all of the new obligations alone, so they begin to look at alternatives. They almost always seem to come to the conclusion that if they took on a partner, they could spread the risk, and they never think about what it will mean to have to get a consensus of opinion from a partner on nearly every aspect of their business life.

Just a few of the issues that often become problematic are: Who on your team does what for whom, and who has priority? Where are you going to advertise and how often? Where will your office and your team be located? Who has final say on hiring if you don't agree on someone? What administrative duties are performed by whom? What marketing areas will you specialize in as a team? Who has priority to the buyer's representative if you have only one? What form of partnership should you have, a C-Corporation, a Limited Liability Company, or what?

> *"The main thought on the minds of mega-producers is to 'generate a lead and make an appointment.'"*

The main thought on the minds of mega-producers is to "generate a lead and make an appointment," and having to deal with all of the distractions stated here and many more is not conducive to your best interests.

Get a Written Contract

If you are still inclined to create a partnership with someone else, it is an absolute must that you have some sort of a written partnership agreement that clearly spells out every detail of your working relationship with each other.

I have offered just a few of the issues that you will need to address in the previous paragraphs, but you will need to go into far more detail, and I cannot stress the importance of good legal counsel enough. What if one of you dies or declares bankruptcy? What if your spouse hates your partner and demands that you either end the partnership or the marriage? What if one of you wants to retire and sell your share of the partnership? There is way more to this than a handshake, and you need to have as many issues covered as you can to avoid a costly court battle over how to settle things.

Many attorneys have boilerplate partnership agreements that cover all of these things; however, you probably can save yourself time and money if you and your new partner or partners sit down first and ask as many of these important questions of each other as you can think of, talk them over openly and fully, and if you are still ready to proceed, then get a referral to an attorney that does this sort of thing for a living. Do not make the mistake of using your attorney-friend, who has no knowledge of this sort of thing as he is probably not skilled at it and may very well miss some extremely critical issues. Be sure to address the issue of "Key-man insurance," which can provide the funds to buy out your partner in the event of an untimely death or disability.

Know Each Other's Strengths and Use Them

Every real estate agent has certain areas of the brokerage business that he or she seems to do with great ease. Depending on how you and your new partner are handling compensation issues, you should have a serious conversation about this and decide where these innate abilities lie and make the most of them.

If you are splitting all of your commissions down the middle, and you are a highly effective buyer's agent while your partner is really good at holding open houses and getting new customers, then you may want to set a routine pattern or job description for this so that each of you brings the maximum benefit of your talents to the partnership.

One of you may have no trepidation about telemarketing while the other one dreads it and would never do it. Obviously this task would fall to the partner that can handle it routinely.

In a partnership, where you have the benefit of pooled net profits, there will be non-selling as well as selling activities that must be routinely performed as well. If one of you is better at creating marketing materials than the other, then this task should be routinely handled by the person with the most skill because the partnership will ultimately benefit the most by it. This also can apply to nonsales issues such as handling legal and accounting matters, creating classified advertising, conducting employment interviews, and managing the administrative staff and other team members whom the partnership has hired.

Sit down and talk through each of these issues and see who is the most comfortable with each; then assign all of the various duties, or agree to do them mutually, such as interviews, and distribute them as evenly as possible. That way, no one feels like he or she is doing too much of the work for too little reward.

After you start to hire additional support such as buyer's representatives, licensed assistants, escrow administrators, and other team members with defined duties, it will be critical that the two of you meet routinely and discuss openly and frankly what each team member is contributing to the team and how well their efforts are being utilized for your mutual benefit.

"The single-biggest reason for the dissolution of these types of partnerships is that one person perceives that the other partner is reaping too much reward for too little contribution."

The single-biggest reason for the dissolution of these types of partnerships is that one person perceives that the other partner is reaping too much reward for too little contribution. This can apply to the partners' personal contribution of time, energy, and money as well as the utilization of the support staff for one partner's benefit more than the other's.

Another potential trouble spot is where two or more agents, who have very different levels of personal production, form a partnership with no clear understanding as to who pays how much for the support staff. It is expected that they will each pay for half of the cost of the administrative staff. After a short time (and it's never more than a short time), the partner with less production sees far too much of the administrative staff's time devoted to the other agent while he or she is footing half the bill. They are reluctant to bring it up as it would rock the boat; but they are feeling more and more frustrated as each day goes by. By the time that they do say something about it, the frustration has turned into anger, and communication about the issue is at an entirely different level than it should be. Words are said that can't be retracted, feelings are hurt, and before long the partnership, and usually a friendship, is over.

Don't let this happen to you. Meet regularly and often and discuss these types of things the minute that you perceive a problem so that they are dealt with long before frustration and anger can arise.

"Meet regularly and often and discuss these types of things the minute that you perceive a problem."

8

The Business Plan

The business plan serves three main purposes: it clearly defines your destination, it serves as a checkpoint of your progress along the way; and it states a defined period of time for you to reach your destination.

For maximum clarity and effectiveness as to where you are going, what specific activities will take place, and how long your journey will be, you will need to do two business plans: a short narrative plan, whereby you state your intentions and when they are to be accomplished; and a year-by-year definitive plan of specific activities that are custom designed by you and committed to in advance.

I would like you to read this next statement very carefully as it may well be the single most important concept in this entire book. *There is a profound difference between a goal and a commitment.*

A goal is an idea or achievement to which you aspire. It is an idealistic destination or a task that will hopefully be performed. It is not a commitment.

> *"A goal is an idea or achievement to which you aspire. It is not a commitment."*

A commitment is a mindset whereby a goal is preaccomplished in the mind the minute that the commitment to do it is made. Failure to achieve it is a nonissue; it is already accomplished in the mind before the task is even begun; then the mind and body simply carry out the duties or acts necessary to see it through.

I have met a large number of mega-producers throughout my career, and to a person, myself included, careful planning and a strong commitment to see those plans through are highly evident in each and every one of them. As you begin to formulate your own business plan by creating goals to be achieved as stepping stones along the way, think through each one carefully and use this thought as a guideline: If it is important enough to become a goal, it is important enough to commit to, so if you won't absolutely commit to doing each task set forth in your business plan, carefully rethink why it is there and change it as necessary. The result will be a business plan that will stretch you to, and maybe just a little past your limits, but one that you will take great pride in accomplishing. Now let's start with a sample narrative business plan.

Narrative Business Plan

2004 through 2008

I currently am achieving approximately $4,000,000 in annual sales volume. I am committing to increase that sales volume to $30,000,000 per year by the end of year five, or 12/31/2008, as follows: $8,000,000 in 2004, $13,000,000 in 2005, $19,000,000 in 2006, $24,000,000 in 2007, and $30,000,000 in 2008.

My current strengths lie in my abilities to generate a large number of new clients by meeting them at my open houses, a high success rate with listing For Sale By Owners, an ability to generate loyalty from my buyers and successfully sell them homes, and a high success rate in generating referrals and repeat business from past and present clients.

While enhancing my skills in these areas, I intend to add to my client base and increase my average sales price by enhancing my skills in the small investment property sales and tax-deferred exchange area and by gaining a market share in the $600,000 to $1,500,000 luxury home market.

I will take three 3-day weekends off: Memorial Day, Independence Day, and Labor Day. I will take the Friday after Thanksgiving off, and I will take 7 days off surrounding the December religious holiday season (Christmas or Hanukah).

My sales volume goals for 2004 are as follows: I will have closed a total of $2 million by 3/31/04; $4.5 million by 6/30/04; $6.5 million by 9/30/04, and $8 million by 12/31/04. Upon meeting or exceeding my 6/30/04 goal, I will invest a minimum of $5,000 in new technology for myself and/or my administrative staff.

I am committing 20 percent of every commission check received to my advertising and marketing fund for 2004, with at least 25 percent of those funds to be used in the luxury home market.

At the earlier of the point where I meet or exceed my annual goal of $8,000,000 in closed sales volume or by February 29, 2004, I will hire a full-time licensed assistant.

By 12/31/03, I will have met with a professional marketing person and our company's marketing department to have them help me create professional marketing brochures and other media and personal items to be used to build my image as a luxury home and small-income property specialist.

2004 Annual Business Plan

Annual sales volume goal is $8,000,000

January 2004

By 1/2/04, I will have my entire list of current and past clients segmented by groups defined by how likely they are to send me referrals, as is taught in the Providence Systems seminars. "A" will equal the "givers" of the world, and I will contact them monthly. "B" will equal people that, once informed several times that I really value their referrals, are likely to become As, and I will contact them every two months. "C" will equal people that I simply am not sure about. They have successfully worked with me before and probably will again, but may or may not be inclined to refer me to someone else. I will contact them twice a year. "D" clients and customers will be deleted. These are people that were or are too demanding, have an agent in the family, etc., and have no reason to work with me, or I don't want to work with them any longer.

By 1/2/04, I will have obtained the names, site addresses, and mailing addresses of a minimum of 400 rental home owners in my marketing area. I will begin a monthly mailing campaign to them followed by as many personal calls to them for which I can get telephone numbers.

I will get and study material on Internal Revenue Code Section 1031 tax-deferred exchanges, as I will need this knowledge with my new income property clients.

By 1/2/04, I also will have identified 250 to 300 luxury homes in my marketing area that are currently in the $600,000 to $1,500,000 price range. I will have all of the current owners researched and identified, and I will begin a methodical monthly marketing campaign to get my name known to them as a luxury home specialist. I will specialize in a given territory of my choosing and learn everything that I can about it, using the narrow and deep concept talked about by Hugh Cornish in Chapter 12.

I will hold an open house the last three Sundays of January, with one open house in the luxury price range.

I will mail a copy of the HUD-1 Settlement Statement to every client and customer that I represented last year.

I will show property to buyers as needed.

February 2004

I will hold open houses four Sundays from 1–4 p.m. with at least one open house being in the luxury home price range.

I will mail to my A group once; my luxury home group twice, and my income property group twice.

I will call my A group to say, "Hello," and remind them about how much I appreciate their referrals.

By 2/29/04, I will hire a licensed assistant to take over all nonproductive tasks such as keybox installation and removal, monthly mailings, and do most of my escrow tasks. He or she will also be a buyer's representative, and I commit to giving him or her a minimum of ten buyer referrals in 2004.

I will show property as needed.

March 2004

I will hold an open house three Sundays from 1–4 p.m. with at least one being in the luxury home price range.

I will mail something of value to my A and B groups and remind them how much I appreciate their referrals. I will thank the A group by phone as well.

I will mail a *comparable sales* brochure mailing and an item of value mailing to my income property and luxury home group.

By 3/31/04, I will start the process to hire a full-time buyer's representative. I will guarantee this person at least 12 buyer referrals in 2004.

I will show property as needed in conjunction with my licensed assistant.

My goal is $2 million in closed sales volume by the end of March.

April 2004
I will mail something of value to my A and C groups and to my luxury home and income property groups.

I will call my A group and some of my B group to say, "Hello."

I will hold an open house three times with at least one in the luxury price range.

I will hire a full-time buyer's representative by month's end with a guarantee of at least 12 buyer referrals. This may mean transitioning my licensed assistant to that position and getting a new licensed assistant.

May 2004
I will hold an open house the first three Sundays of the month and take the Memorial Day weekend off.

I will mail 9-volt batteries to my A group, my luxury home group, and to my income property group with a reminder to change the one in their smoke detector.

I will call my A group to remind them that I always have time for *their* referrals.

I will show property as necessary in conjunction with my team.

June 2004

I will update my listing presentation brochure, to include any new testimonial letters that I have received.

I will spend up to $7,000 on new technology for myself and/or my team.

I will hold three open houses including at least one in the luxury price range.

I will mail something of value to my A and B group and *comparables* to my luxury and income property groups.

I will call as many of my luxury home group as possible to say hello.

I will show property in conjunction with my team.

My sales volume goal is $4.5 million in closed production by the end of this month.

July 2004

I will take the July 4th weekend off.

I will hold an open house the last three Sundays of the month from 1–4 p.m. with at least one in the luxury price range.

I will mail something of value to my A group and my income property and luxury home groups.

I will call my A group and remind them that I always have time for their referrals.

I will show property in conjunction with my team.

August 2004

I will hold an open house three times with at least one being in the luxury price range.

I will mail out to all groups.

I will call the A and B groups to say hello and ask whether they are getting my mailings.

I will set up all of my contact groups into different databases according to special issues or occupations such as pet owners, motorcyclists, attorneys, financial planners, and so on.

I will show property in conjunction with my team.

September 2004

I will take the Labor Day weekend off.

I will hold three open houses with at least one in the luxury home price range.

I will mail something of value to my A group, and I will mail comparables to my income property and luxury home groups.

I will call my A group just to say, "Hello," and to remind them of the importance of their referrals.

I will show property in conjunction with my team.

I will evaluate my overall business development year-to-date. If warranted, I will begin the process of hiring an escrow administrator. When I do hire the escrow administrator, I will have the licensed assistant perform all off-site nonselling activities and give him or her more buyer referrals or co-listings.

My sales volume goal is $6.5 million in closed production by the end of this month.

October 2004

I will hold open houses three times with at least one being in the luxury home price range.

I will mail out something of value to my A and B group and to my income property and luxury home groups.

I will call my A and B group to say, "Hello," ask about summer vacations, and remind them that I always have time for their referrals and really appreciate them.

I will show property in conjunction with my team.

November 2004

I will hold an open house the first two weeks of the month with at least one in the luxury price range.

I will mail Happy Thanksgiving cards to my A and B list and to selected people on my income property and luxury home groups that I have come to know on a more personal basis.

I will call my A group and wish them and their families a Happy Thanksgiving.

I will call selected people from my luxury group and my income property group to wish them a Happy Thanksgiving. These calls will be to people from those groups that I have either met personally or talked with extensively on the telephone or with whom I've built a relationship.

December 2004

I will hold open houses the first two weeks of the month with both homes being in the luxury home price range if possible.

I will mail a Happy Holidays card to all of my groups by December 10 to avoid the holiday mail crunch. This note will either say how much I appreciated their support (for a referral), their business (if they bought or sold through me or my team), or that I look forward to doing business with them next year (if they didn't do anything with me this year).

I will set time aside to be alone first and then time with my team to evaluate our individual and team performance for the past year. I will make any necessary adjustments to fine tune each member of the team as well as the team as a whole.

I will assess my new role as the rainmaker or business development specialist. I will also assess the strengths and weaknesses of each team member and then have a private conversation with them about any weak areas. Remember to always praise in public and criticize in private.

This will also be a time to assess the business climate and compare it to the workload of my existing staff for purposes of deciding whether or not to add staff and when.

My sales volume goal by the end of December is $8 million in closed production.

2005 Annual Business Plan

Annual sales volume goal is $13,000,000.

This, the second year of my journey to becoming a mega-producer, will be one of maintaining my ever-growing base income through refinement of my skills and those of my team members, while I leverage my talents by further additions to my team.

My direct involvement in holding open houses will wane dramatically as I continue to acquire more and more new clients by referral and repeat business and through the efforts of my team members.

It will be a year of advanced courses in investment property sales and exchanges as the relationships with my income property group start to mature into new business, and I will need to refine my marketing skills in both the income property and luxury home areas as I will also begin to see some listings and buyers result from my last year's efforts in both of those areas.

January 2005

I will spend every other Saturday and two Sundays doing drop-bys to my A groups' homes to keep in touch and stay on top of referrals.

I will hold an open house for a luxury home on the last Sunday of the month.

I will send a copy of the HUD-1 Escrow Closing Statement to all customers and clients that my team and I worked with last year.

I will send an item of value to my A and B groups and to my luxury and income property groups that did not get a HUD-1 closing statement.

I will call my A group to say, "Happy New Year," and to check in for referrals.

I will show property as necessary in conjunction with my team.

I will seek out new tapes, books, or CDs about income property sales and exchanges, especially mini-storages and retail shopping centers. This is the beginning of niche marketing within the income property sector.

February 2005

I will hold one luxury home open house on a Sunday from 1–5 p.m.

I will do two Saturday and two Sunday pop-by's to past clients' homes to leave a forget-me-not and to check in for referrals.

I will mail comparables to my A and B groups and my luxury home and income property groups.

I will call my A group to just say, "Hello," and to remind them that I always have time for their referrals.

I will get the title company to get me a list of all of the mini-storage facility owners in my marketing area so that I may put them into my contact management program and start a quarterly mailing program to them.

I will show property to buyers in conjunction with my team as the need arises.

I will hire a second buyer's representative and have him or her fully trained by month's end.

March 2005

I will take a weekend off this month.

I will hold one luxury home open house on a Sunday from 1–4 p.m.

I will do pop-by's on two Saturdays and two Sundays.

I will call my A and B groups to say, "Hello," and check in for referrals, and I will call my luxury and income groups to see whether anyone requires my services.

I will mail out an item of value to my A and B groups and to my luxury home and income property groups.

I will finish all necessary research on the mini-storage ownership records and have the data entered into my computer by the end of this month.

I will show property in conjunction with my team.

My sales volume goal for this quarter is $3.5 million in closed production.

April 2005

I will hold one luxury open house from 1–4 p.m. on a Sunday.

I will mail out an item of value to my A and C groups and to my luxury home and income property groups.

I will call my A group to check in for referrals and tell them that I always have time for their referrals.

I will send an introductory letter to my mini-storage group.

I will show property in conjunction with my team.

May 2005

I will hold one open house for a luxury home the first Sunday of the month.

I will mail something of value to my A group, and I will mail comparables to my luxury group and my income property group, which now includes my mini-storage group.

I will call my mini-storage group to introduce myself.

I will call my A group to ask how they are, what they have planned for the Memorial Day holiday, and to see about any referrals.

I will do pop-by's to my A group on two Saturdays and one Sunday.

I will show property to buyers in conjunction with my team.

June 2005

I will assess the market, and if reasonable to do so, I will hire another combination licensed assistant and buyer's representative to work approximately a half-day on each as necessary.

I will mail something of value to my A and B groups and to my income property and luxury home groups, letting them know of my team's success, how they have helped, and how much I appreciate their referrals.

I will hold one luxury home open house, and I will send an invitation to all of the neighbors.

I will call my A and B groups, and I will call my income property and luxury home groups to see whether they got the comparables from last month.

I will show property to buyers in conjunction with my team.

My sales volume goal by the end of June is $7,500,000 in closed production.

July 2005

I will hold one luxury home open house late in the month.

I will take the July 4th weekend off.

I will mail something of value to my A group and to my income property and my luxury home group.

I will call my A group and wish them a Happy 4th of July and thank them for their referrals.

I will do pop-by's two Saturdays.

I will send out invitations to my client appreciation picnic.

I will show property to buyers in conjunction with my team.

August 2005

I will hold a luxury home open house the first Sunday of the month.

I will have a client appreciation picnic the second week of the month; either at my home, if it is big enough, or at a park or Country Club that I will reserve. This will include my A and B group, luxury homeowners with whom I have built a relationship, and any local income property owners with whom I have built a relationship.

I will call my A clients early in the month to see whether they are coming to the picnic and to check in for referrals.

I will mail all of my groups something of value.

I will do pop-by's to my A group and selected people from my luxury home group on two Saturdays.

I will show property to buyers in conjunction with my team.

September 2005

I will take the Labor Day weekend off.

I will hold two luxury home open houses on the last two Sundays of the month, and I will send invitations to 100 of the neighbors.

I will mail something of value to my A group and comparables to my income property and luxury home group.

I will call my A group to ask how their Labor Day weekend was, to check in for referrals, and to see how they enjoyed the picnic if they came.

I will do pop-by's on two Saturdays to my A group and to select people from my luxury home group.

I will show property to buyers in conjunction with my team.

My sales volume goal by the end of September is $10,000,000 in closed production.

October 2005

I will hold two luxury home open houses on Sundays, with invitations to the surrounding neighbors.

I will mail something of value to my A and B groups and to my income property and luxury home groups.

I will call my A group to tell them how much I appreciate their support of my working-by-referral program, and I will call select people from my income property group and luxury home group.

I will do pop-by's on two Saturdays to my A group.

I will show property to buyers in conjunction with my team.

November 2005

I will take a 4-day holiday at Thanksgiving.

I will hold one luxury home open house the first week of the month.

I will mail Happy Thanksgiving cards to my A and B list and to selected people in my income property and luxury home groups with whom I have developed a relationship .

I will call my A group and wish them and their families a Happy Thanksgiving and to thank them for their referrals.

I will call selected people from my luxury group and income property group to wish them a Happy Thanksgiving. This will be limited to people with whom I have built some type of relationship.

I will show property to buyers in conjunction with my team.

December 2005

I will hold one luxury home open house the first Sunday in December.

I will mail a Happy Holidays card to all of my groups by December 10 to avoid the holiday mail crunch. This note will either say how much I appreciated their support this last year (for a referral), their business (if they bought or sold through me or my team), or that I look forward to doing business with them next year (if they didn't do anything with me this year).

I will review and change or delete people from all groups as necessary.

I will set time aside to be alone first and then time with my team to evaluate our individual and our team performance for the past year and to make any necessary adjustments to fine tune each member of the team as well as the team as a whole.

I will take my escrow administrator to lunch and ask her to assess the team's and my strengths and weaknesses.

I will have a private meeting with each team member to assess his or her performance and to ask for constructive feedback.

I will assess the business climate and, if appropriate, I will make plans to add staff as necessary. This will include another buyer's representative and a telemarketer. I will identify at least four subdivisions in which I want to gain market share and hire the telemarketer to concentrate in those subdivisions.

My sales volume goal by the end of December is $13,000,000 in closed production.

2006 ANNUAL BUSINESS PLAN

Annual sales volume goal is $19,000,000

If I have not obtained a broker's license, I will start to do so the last quarter of this year. I will also take one of the courses necessary for the Certified Commercial Investment Member (CCIM) designation from the National Association of REALTORS®.

I will set money aside to pay for one-half of the cost of professional designations such as the Certified Residential Specialist (CRS) for my buyer's representatives as a sort of bonus.

The telemarketer will be creating many more listings in the bread-and-butter areas as well as the luxury home market for me, so I will need to pay particular attention to having enough licensed assistants and other agents from the office that I work at to hold open houses to keep the sellers satisfied.

I will take every Sunday off this year unless I am asked specifically by a client of mine to show them property or to take a listing.

January 2006

I will send a HUD-1 Escrow Closing Statement to all customers and clients that my team and I worked with last year.

I will mail something of value to my A and B groups that did not get a HUD-1 statement and comparables to my luxury home and income property groups.

I will spend two Saturdays doing drop-by's to my A group and two Saturdays showing property. I can increase the number of Saturday drop-by's, but I can't decrease it. It is too important in the lead-generation process.

I will call my A group to ask whether they had a fun New Year's Eve and to check in for referrals.

February 2006

I will do pop-by's on at least two Saturdays to my A group and to select luxury home group members.

I will call my A group to say, "Hello," to remind them that I always have time for their referrals, and to say that I appreciate them very much.

I will mail comparables to my A group and to my income property and luxury home groups.

I will show property to buyers in conjunction with my team.

March 2006

I will take the entire first weekend off this month.

I will do pop-by's to my A group on at least two Saturdays.

I will call my A and B groups to say, "Hello," and to remind them that I always have time for their referrals. I will call my luxury home group and my income property group and ask whether any of them need my services.

I will mail an item of value to my A and B groups and to my luxury home and income property groups.

I will show property to buyers in conjunction with my team.

My sales volume goal for the end of March is $4,000,000.

April 2006

I will mail an item of value to my A and C groups and to my income property and luxury home groups.

I will call my A group to check in and to tell them that I always have time for their referrals.

I will add 50–100 homes to my database that are in the $1,000,000 + price range.

I will do pop-by's to my A group at least two Saturdays.

I will show property to buyers in conjunction with my team.

May 2006

I will mail something of value to my A group, and I will mail comparables to my luxury home group and my income property groups.

I will mail an introductory letter and sample marketing materials to my new $1,000,000 + group the first week in May; then I will follow up with a telephone call the second week.

I will do pop-by's to my A group and select people in my luxury home group on at least two Saturdays.

I will call my A group and select people in my luxury home group and income property group to see what they have planned for the Memorial Day holiday and to see about referrals.

I will show property to buyers in conjunction with my team.

I will take a 4-day weekend in conjunction with the Memorial Day weekend.

June 2006

I will meet with each team member to evaluate the market, their role on the team, and how effectively they are working as a team member. After all meetings are complete, I will evaluate the team as a whole and make changes in duties and responsibilities as necessary.

I will mail something of value to my A and B groups and to my luxury home and income property groups.

I will call my A and B groups to check in for referrals, to thank them for their support, and to tell them how much I appreciate it.

I will call my income property groups to ask whether the increased values that they have experienced recently have given them enough equity in their property to either exchange it for a larger property or a different kind of investment property; or to possibly think about refinancing their existing property to pull out some cash to use as the down payment on another one just like it.

I will show property to buyers in conjunction with my team.

My sales volume goal at the end of June is $10,000,000.

July 2006

I will make July 4th a four-day holiday.

I will mail something of value to my A group, income property group, and luxury home group and wish them a Happy Independence Day.

I will call my A group and ask how their summer is going so far and see whether they have any referrals for me.

I will send invitations to my annual client appreciation picnic to my A group and to select members of my income property and luxury home group.

I will do pop-by's on two Saturdays.

I will show property to buyers in conjunction with my team.

August 2006

I will call my A and B clients to see how they are, what vacations they have taken so far, and to see about referrals.

I will mail out something of value to my A and C groups and to my income property and luxury home groups.

I will do pop-by's on at least two Saturdays this month.

I will have my annual client appreciation picnic.

I will show property in conjunction with my team.

September 2006

I will take the Labor Day weekend off.

I will mail something of value to my A group and comparables to my luxury home and income property groups.

I will call my A group to see how their Labor Day weekend went and to check in for referrals.

I will do pop-by's at least two Saturdays of the month; more if possible. This will be to my A group and to select luxury home owners in my group.

I will show property in conjunction with my team.

My sales volume goal for the end of the month is $16,500,000.

October 2006

I will mail something of value to my A and B groups and to my income property and luxury home groups.

I will call my A group to remind them how important their support of my referral program is and how much I appreciate them.

I will do pop-by's to my A group and to selected luxury home owners in my group on at least two Saturdays.

I will show property to buyers in conjunction with my team.

November 2006

I will take a 4-day holiday at Thanksgiving.

I will mail Happy Thanksgiving cards to my A and B groups and to selected people in my income property and luxury home groups with whom I have developed relationships.

I will call my A group to wish them and their families a Happy Thanksgiving and to thank them for their referrals.

I will call "selected" people from my luxury group and income property group with whom I have built a relationship with to wish them a Happy Thanksgiving.

I will show property to buyers in conjunction with my team.

December 2006

I will mail a Happy Holidays card to all of my groups by December 10 to avoid the holiday mail crunch. This note will either say how much I appreciated their support this last year (for a referral), their business (if they bought or sold through me or my team), or that I look forward to doing business with them next year (if they didn't do anything with me this year).

I will review and change or delete people from all groups as necessary.

I will set time aside to be alone first and then time with my team to evaluate our individual and out team performance for the past year and to make necessary adjustments to fine tune each member of the team as well as the team as a whole.

I will take my escrow administrator to lunch and ask her to assess the team's and my strengths and weaknesses.

I will have a private meeting with each team member to assess their performance and to ask for constructive feedback.

I will assess the business climate and, if appropriate, I will make plans to adjust the size of the staff as needed. In order to expand my market presence, I will look very closely at adding another telemarketer and another buyer's representative if appropriate.

I will do pop-by's the first two Saturdays of the month to my A group.

I will call my A group and wish them Happy Holidays and ask what their plans are for the coming year.

I will show property to buyers in conjunction with my team.

I will take the Christmas week off as vacation.

My sales volume goal for the year end is $19,000,000.

2007 Annual Business Plan

Annual sales volume goal is $24,000,000.

I now have an escrow coordinator that handles my escrows and listings, four buyer's representatives to handle most of the buyer-referrals that I get, two licensed assistants to handle listing maintenance and hold open houses, and two telemarketers to obtain listing appointments for me.

My time this year will be spent almost entirely taking listings, presenting offers, and seeing and calling past clients and people in my groups to develop new and repeat business for me and my team.

I will take one full weekend a month off, plus another Sunday a month, and five 3-day weekends. In addition, I will take two 1-week vacations—one during July and one at Christmas.

January 2007

I will spend at least two Saturdays a month doing drop-by's to my A clients' homes to keep in touch and stay on top of referrals.

I will send a copy of the HUD-1 Escrow Closing Statement to all customers and clients that my team worked with last year.

I will send an item of value to my A and B groups and to my income property and luxury home groups.

I will call my A group to say Happy New Year and to check in for referrals.

I will show property in conjunction with my team.

February 2007

I will do pop-by's to my A group at least two Saturdays of the month.

I will mail comparables to my A and B groups and to my income property and luxury home groups.

I will call my A group just to say, "Hello," and remind them that I always have time for their referrals.

I will get all of the information that I can get on mini-storage sales in other states and share that with my mini-storage group.

I will show property to buyers in conjunction with my team. I will handle all investment property buyers personally.

March 2007

I will take two weekends off this month.

I will do pop-by's to my A group and to select people in my luxury home group on at least two Saturdays.

I will mail an item of value to my A and B groups and to my income property and luxury home groups.

I will call my A group to say, "Hello."

I will show property to buyers in conjunction with my team.

My sales volume goal for the end of this month is $5,500,000.

April 2007

I will mail an item of value to my A and C groups and mail comparables to my income property and luxury home groups.

I will call my A group to check in for referrals.

I will do pop-by's to my A group and to select members of my luxury home group.

I will show property to buyers in conjunction with my team.

May 2007

I will take a 4-day weekend in conjunction with the Memorial Day holiday.

I will mail something of value to my A and B group and to my income property group.

I will call my mini-storage group to see whether they have any interest in acquiring a mini-storage facility in another state or out of their immediate area.

I will call my A group to ask how they are, what they have planned for the Memorial Day holiday, and to see about referrals.

I will do pop-by's to my A group the first two Saturdays of this month.

I will show property to buyers in conjunction with my team.

I will sign up to attend the first CCIM course in July.

June 2007

I will assess the market against the overall workload and efficiency of my current team. I will then decide what, if any, action I need to take in adding another person to the team.

I will meet with each team member to assess their personal effectiveness and the team's effectiveness and make adjustments and provide training and guidance as necessary.

I will mail something of value to my A group and to my luxury group, letting them know of my team's success and thanking them for their part in it.

I will call my income property and luxury home groups to see whether they got the comparables that I sent last month.

I will show property to buyers in conjunction with my team.

My sales volume goal by the end of June is $13,000,000.

July 2007

I will make a 4-day weekend out of the July 4th Holiday.

I will mail something of value to my A and B groups and to my income property and luxury home groups.

I will call my A group and select people in my luxury home group and wish them a Happy 4th of July and ask what they have planned. I will also remind them of my picnic next month.

I will do pop-by's at least two Saturdays of the month.

I will send out invitations to my client appreciation picnic.

I will attend the first CCIM class wherever in the United States that it is being held.

I will show property to buyers in conjunction with my team.

August 2007

I will have my client appreciation picnic the second weekend of the month. This group will include my A and B clients and select people in my luxury home and local income property owner groups.

I will call all of my A clients early in the month to see whether they are coming to the picnic and to check in for referrals.

I will mail my A and C groups something of value and comparables to my income property and luxury groups.

I will do pop-by's at least two Saturdays of the month.

I will show property to buyers in conjunction with my team.

September 2007

I will take the Labor Day weekend off, including an extra day.

I will mail something of value to my A group and to my income and luxury home groups.

I will call my A group to ask how their Labor Day weekend was, to check in for referrals, and to see how they enjoyed the picnic, if they came.

I will do pop-by's the last two Saturdays of the month.

I will show property to buyers in conjunction with my team.

My sales volume goal by the end of September is $18,500,000.

October 2007

I will mail something of value to my A and B groups and to my luxury home and income property groups.

I will call my A group and tell them how much I appreciate their support of my working-by-referral program, and I will call select people from my income property and luxury home groups and do the same.

I will do pop-by's at least two Saturdays to my A group.

I will show property to buyers in conjunction with my team.

(*Optional*) I may have a costume party on Halloween at my home or an appropriate place. If I do, I will send out invitations early in the month and ask about it when I call.

November 2007

I will take a 4-day holiday at Thanksgiving.

I will mail Happy Thanksgiving cards to my A and B list, to selected people in my luxury home group, and to local owners in my income property group with whom I have developed a relationship.

I will call my A group and select people from my income property and luxury home group, wish them and their families a Happy Thanksgiving, and thank them for their referrals and their business this year.

I will show property to buyers in conjunction with my team.

December 2007

I will mail a Happy Holidays card to all of my groups by December 10 to avoid the holiday mail crunch. This note will either say how much I appreciated their support this year (for a referral) or their business (if they bought or sold through me or my team). Anyone in my database who hasn't either referred someone to me or done business with me by the end of the fourth year of being a B or C in my database will be eliminated at year end.

I will set time to be alone first and then time with my team to evaluate our individual and our team performance for the past year and to make any necessary adjustments to fine tune each member of the team as well as the team as a whole.

I will take my escrow administrator to lunch and ask her to assess the team's and my strengths and weaknesses.

I will have a private meeting with each team member to assess his or her performance and to ask for constructive feedback.

I will meet with someone from my company's marketing department and have them assess my team's as well as my personal marketing and sales brochures and plan.

I will show property to buyers in conjunction with my team.

I will take the Christmas week off as vacation.

My sales volume goal by the end of December is $24,000,000.

2008 Annual Business Plan

Annual sales volume goal is $30,000,000.

This is the last year of my initial 5-year business plan, so it is time to start constructing the next 5 years. I will have the next five-year plan done by March 31 of this year.

This year, I will take the second and third Certified Commercial Investment Member (CCIM) courses somewhere in the United States.

This year, I will invest in at least two rental homes for my retirement and, depending on the business climate, I may buy a more upscale home to live in as my primary residence or purchase a vacation home in the Napa Valley.

I now have one escrow administrator, five buyer's representatives, two licensed assistants, and two telemarketers. By the end of January, I will assess where my business is in conjunction with the current demands on it by customers and clients and the direction of the current market conditions and trends. If it is appropriate, I will add staff as necessary.

I will take every Sunday off this year unless a client calls me, and I will take five 3-day weekends and a 2-week vacation.

My sales volume goal by the end of 2008 is $30,000,000 in closed production.

January 2008

I will do pop-by's to my A group and to certain people in my luxury home group every Saturday.

I will mail something of value to my A and B groups and to my income property and luxury home group.

I will call all of my A group to see whether they had a nice New Year holiday.

I will schedule my second CCIM class for March.

I will mail a HUD-1 Escrow Closing Statement to every client who bought or sold a property through my team last year.

I will show property in conjunction with my team.

February 2008

I will mail comparables to my A group and to my income property and luxury home group.

I will call my A group and my income property and luxury home group to thank them for the referrals that they sent me last year and to say how much their support means to the success of my team.

I will do drop-by's every Saturday to my A group and to select people from my luxury home group.

I will show property in conjunction with my team.

March 2008

I will mail something of value to my A and B group and to my luxury home and my income property groups.

I will call my A group and select people in my luxury home group to say, "hello," and keep in touch. I will mention that I always have time for their referrals.

I will do pop-by's every Saturday to my A group and to select people from my luxury home group.

I will attend the second CCIM class somewhere in the United States.

I will show property in conjunction with my team.

My sales volume goal for the first quarter is $7 million.

April 2008

I will mail out an item of value about income taxes to my A group and to my luxury home and income property group.

I will call my A group to say, "Hello," and to check in for referrals.

I will call or write to each member of my mini-storage group to see whether they wish to sell, exchange, or acquire another mini-storage project.

I will show property in conjunction with my team.

I will take a 3-day weekend this month.

I will purchase an investment property this month.

May 2008

I will mail comparables to my A and B groups and to my income property and luxury home groups.

I will call my A group and select people from my luxury home group and income property group to check in for referrals and to see what they have planned for the Memorial Day holiday.

I will do pop-by's to my A group on three Saturdays.

I will show property in conjunction with my team.

I will have my whole team and their families over to my house for a Memorial Day barbeque.

June 2008

I will mail something of value to my A group and to my luxury home group.

I will do pop-by's to my A group on three Saturdays.

I will call my A and B group and select people from my income property and luxury home group to say, "Hello," ask what their summer plans are, and see whether they got the comparables that I sent.

I will show property in conjunction with my team.

I will assess the current and foreseeable market and the current demands on my existing team and add staff if appropriate.

My sales volume goal by the end of June is $15.5 million.

July 2008

I will make a 3-day weekend out of the July 4th holiday.

I will call my A and B groups and select people from my income property and luxury home groups and ask how their holiday weekend was, to check in for referrals, and to remind them how much I appreciate them and the referrals that they send to me.

I will mail something of value to my A and B groups and to my luxury home group.

I will do pop-by's on three Saturdays to my A group and to select people from my luxury home group.

I will register for the third CCIM class in August.

I will show property to buyers in conjunction with my team.

August 2008

I will attend the third CCIM class.

I will do pop-by's to my A group and to select people from my luxury home group on three Saturdays.

I will mail comparables to my A group and to my luxury home and income property group early in the month.

I will call my A group and my luxury home and income property groups to ask how they feel about what the prices of their real estate are doing and to thank them again for their referrals.

I will show property to buyers in conjunction with my team.

September 2008

I will take a 1-week vacation in conjunction with the Labor Day holiday.

During the third week of the month, I will mail invitations to my Halloween costume party set for late October to my A group, to select people from my luxury home group, and local owners of my income property group whom I have come to know well.

During the fourth week of the month, I will call my A group, select people from my luxury home group, and local owners from my income property group to see whether they got invitations to my Halloween party and to thank them again for the referrals and the business.

I will do pop-by's to my A group on three Saturdays.

I will show property to buyers in conjunction with my team.

My sales volume goal for the end of September is $18.5 million.

October 2008

I will take a 3-day weekend the last week of the month.

I will buy my second rental property by the end of the month.

I will set the first Wednesday of the month aside to start to create my next 5-year business plan.

I will do pop-by's to my A group on the first three Saturdays of the month.

I will mail something of value to my A and B groups and to my luxury home and income property groups.

I will call my A group, select people from my luxury home group, and my income property groups to see who is coming to the Halloween party and to thank them for their business and their referrals.

I will show property to buyers in conjunction with my team.

November 2008

I will take a 4-day holiday at Thanksgiving.

I will mail Happy Thanksgiving cards to my A and B groups and to my luxury home and income property groups.

I will call my A group and select people from my luxury home group to wish them a Happy Thanksgiving and to thank them for their referrals.

I will do pop-by's to my A group the first three Saturdays of the month.

I will show property to buyers in conjunction with my team.

December 2008

I will set the first weekend aside to finish my next 5-year business plan. This will include an evaluation of each team member that will lead to one-on-one discussions with each of them.

I will call my A group and wish them Happy Holidays.

I will mail a Happy Holidays card to all of my groups by December 10 to avoid the holiday mail crunch. This card will either say how much I appreciated their support this last year (if they gave me a referral), their business (if they bought or sold through me or my team), or that I look forward to doing business with them next year (if they didn't do anything with me this year).

My B and C list will be analyzed each year, and if someone hasn't either done business with me or my team within five consecutive years, they will be deleted from the group.

I will meet with each member of the team to evaluate them and get feedback from them as to what will make the team better.

I will have lunch with my escrow administrator and have her assess the team's and my strengths and weaknesses.

I will assess where I want to take the team and my personal production over the next five years and make plans to add staff accordingly.

I will show property in conjunction with my team.

I will take a 1-week vacation at Christmas or Hanukah.

My sales volume goal by the end of December is $30,000,000.

Day-to-Day Operations

Your Role as the "RAINMAKER"

By now, it should have become very clear to you that you are no longer primarily in the real estate business. You are now in the lead-generation business, and real estate brokerage is the arena that you have chosen to work within to generate those precious Leads, which will be converted into satisfied lifetime clients and income for you and your team.

Prior to making a decision to become a mega-producer, you wore many hats. You did escrow work; met inspectors, appraisers, and a host of other people at properties that you had listed or sold; showed property to buyers; took floor time; held open houses; and did all of the other things that the average real estate agent did. Now, you have specially assigned team members to do those things for you, and your task, simply put, is to generate business for you and your team.

The mega-producer system doesn't call for you to take on this sometimes daunting task all by yourself; that's what specialization and delegation is all about and where the true value of your team comes in. You will have licensed assistants holding open houses for you. They will meet both buyers and sellers, and these leads will be passed on to you to disseminate to your specialized team members at your discretion. You may have one or more telemarketers

"The mega-producer system doesn't call for you to take on this sometimes daunting task all by yourself."

getting you a steady stream of listing appointments. These, too, will be handled by you or your team at your discretion. Be very sure that these Telemarketers strictly abide by the rules set by the National Do

Not Call List, as there can be major sanctions against you and your company for violations.

You personally will be contacting the people in your database on a regular basis, and this will generate many, many listing appointments and buyer showings. You will have one or more buyer's representatives on your team, and you will turn many, if not most, of these buyer leads over to so that you can spend your time doing what you do the best—generating more business.

By concentrating on lead generation and delegating most of the buyer-oriented tasks and the listing-maintenance tasks to your team, you will reap a large portion of the commission from far more listings and sales than you would the old-fashioned way. This is essentially leveraging yourself and your talents to their maximum efficiency, and it is clearly the way to start growing a business instead of selling real estate.

Delegation

Real estate agents, especially the really good ones, are not very good at delegating tasks to other people. I was certainly that way as a new agent and carried that through when I opened my own company. I nearly drove myself and everyone around me nuts for about 3 years until I finally learned to hire high-quality people and trust them to do what they were asked to do.

> *"As the boss . . . your job is to hire high-quality people for your team, give them clear and specific duties and responsibilities, and hold them accountable for their flawless execution."*

As the boss, and you are the boss, independent contractor issue aside, your job is to hire high-quality people for your team, give them clear and specific duties and responsibilities, and hold them accountable for their flawless execution. At first, you will feel frustrated when something isn't done just the way that you like it, or more time is taken to accomplish a certain task than you feel is appropriate. You will be very tempted to just jump in and do it yourself, and you will have to hold yourself in check and work with your team members to bring them up to speed.

This is a normal growth experience. If you are ever going to truly utilize the efforts of other people to help attain your goals, you are going to have to go through this process. Grin and bear it; it isn't easy, but it simply must be done.

You will find that the process of getting your team up to speed will be shortened considerably by specialization and effective delegation. Someone that is highly efficient at creating flyers and putting them in your listings and placing and removing keyboxes may be very uncomfortable showing a buyer those same properties, so work through the various tasks that a position calls for and talk through them very carefully with a new team member before you hire that person on a permanent basis.

Literally every task that is necessary from the cold-call that gets a listing appointment through the listing-maintenance process, creating and placing advertising, showing properties to buyers, writing and presenting offers, conducting escrows, and the after-escrow follow-up process needs to be carefully thought through as to who on your team is the most capable of doing it. Then you need to assign each task to one or more specific people. You must carefully and patiently train them in your way of doing things and then empower them to do the assigned tasks and hold them accountable for the outcome. Patience is a virtue here, as your way may be different, even to a seasoned agent.

Prioritizing Your Time

As you read through the 5-year business plan, you probably noticed that each and every month has both new and repetitive activities that must be done. It is understood that each of you will alter the basic plan given in this book to fit your exact style and meet *"One of the basics is a keen sense of the value of their time."* your personal goals; however, basics are basics. When you read the interviews with the four mega-producers whom I interview in Chapter 12, you will see each one of them strictly adheres to certain basics. One of the basics is a keen sense of the value of their time.

Two true facts that don't change are as follows: The more money that you earn, the more your time is worth on an hourly basis; and the larger your team becomes, the more money it costs you to operate on an hourly basis. Look at the examples that follow to get an idea of what a wasted hour or two can cost you. Assume that you work a 50-hour week 52 weeks a year.

$4,000,000 annual sales × 3% (commission)
= $120,000 / 2600 hours = $46 an hour.

$30,000,000 annual sales × 3% (commission)
= $900,000 / 2600 hours = $346 an hour.

At the same time that your gross income is rising as you build your team, so are your monthly expenses. It is easy to see how an hour wasted here and there can end up costing you a small fortune at year end.

Now stop for a minute and think; this is not to say that you have to get crazy about this whole thing. You should schedule time off as I have done in the five-year business plan. If you don't, *"You should schedule time off . . . If you don't, you'll burn out after a short time."* you'll burn out after a short time, and the whole thing is a moot point; that's the whole point of building a team, so that it is still in full operation while you are away on that well-earned vacation.

The idea is that there are $9 an hour activities and $300 an hour activities. Place your personal priorities where they were meant to be, which is generating leads, taking listings, and representing buyers. *Note:* You should take all listings in your name, and you should work only with buyers who are personal in nature to you such as family, past clients whom you sold to personally, and so on. Most of the other buyers should be delegated to buyer's representatives, except for high-end buyers and influential people.

Whether you use a PDA or an appointment book, you have to get in the habit of planning your next day's activities and the activities of your team before you go to bed each night. Sit quietly and think of each task that needs to be done the next day and write it down; this should even include picking up your laundry and other personal things that can be assigned to others.

After you are finished, put the name of the person the task has been assigned to at the right of the task. When you have all of the tasks noted that must be completed, number each task by its importance, make a list for each person, and put it on their desks first thing each morning. If all of your team has a database program, you can just make a spreadsheet and email it to each of them every night.

Each team member will, of course, have their own daily agenda, but by doing this yourself each night, you will add to their effectiveness as it relates to your team in a very noticeable way.

When you are going to be away, you will need to have a team member who can do this for you. The obvious person is the escrow coordinator as he or she knows the status of each escrow and is easily reachable for direction by the other team members.

Team Meetings

Pick a day of the week that works best for you and have a regularly scheduled team meeting. Nikki Mehalic has a regular meeting with her team every Wednesday morning at 8:30 sharp.

Have an agenda prepared. Your escrow administrator or one of your licensed assistants can do this. From time to time, have a guest speaker who can impart some meaningful information that your team will find helpful. This speaker might be a tax attorney, a CPA, an insurance broker, one of your developer clients, or anyone else whom you feel has something meaningful to offer your team. *Caution:* You will get requests from nonessential people who are trying to sell you and/or your team something that you don't want or need. If this happens, just tell them that your team makes the decision about speakers and that you will present them and their product to the team for a decision and get back to them.

If you have a guest speaker, they should be first on the meeting agenda so that you can dismiss them after they are through, and you can speak privately with your team. The remainder of your agenda should have reports from each segment of your team, such as buyer's status reports, listing status reports, escrow status reports, For Sale By Owner status reports, and farm area status reports by percentage of market share.

Team meetings are a good time to talk about market conditions, what segments of the market are active or slow, such as luxury homes or a certain area that has seen a bunch of new listings in a short time.

From time to time there will be personality clashes, team members who are underperforming, important escrow matters that were missed or late due to carelessness, and so on. Right after the meeting is a good time to meet privately with any team member who needs counseling. Remember the old adage that says "praise in public—criticize in private." It is *never* a good idea to criticize someone for a shortcoming in front of other people.

> *"Remember the old adage that says 'praise in public—criticize in private.'"*

You often can get a lot of mileage out of your team meetings by asking, right at the end of the meeting, "Well, what direction should we head in now?" If you are careful in the selection of your team, you will hire some incredible talent, and they love a chance to shine. It will amaze you at the insight that they have into different segments of the market which you haven't seen.

Be very careful to follow up on a good idea that is expressed during these sessions as there is a dual benefit. Your team member gets a chance to shine and be acknowledged for his or her intuition and perception, and your entire team often gets a new opportunity for increased earnings from these little afterthought sessions.

Handling Interruptions

Your daily schedule can and will be interrupted in several ways. As time is money, these interruptions can be very costly. If one of your team members calls you or comes in to see you while you are in the office and says that they or we have a problem, ask them for a short version of the problem. When they are finished, ask them what they think the solution is. On most occasions, they will be right. If this is true, tell them so and compliment them on their analytical skills. This empowers them, makes them surer of themselves the next time a situation arises, and makes them a more valuable team member.

If another agent in your office stops you and wants to chat, you have a decision to make. If you are in the mood and nothing is pressing right at the moment, stop and talk for a few minutes, but if this agent is one of the hangers-on whom so many real estate offices tend to hire and who is looking to you for a quick-fix solution to the age-old problem—they want business without working for it—be as polite as necessary, but cut it short. They won't do what you tell them anyway, as it would require work and possibly rejection of some sort.

Another form of interruption is the high-maintenance client who feels that you owe him or her a phone call or personal visit every few hours of every day. Every one of you can recall, usually with a shudder, at least five of these characters; I know that I can!

The new cellular telephones that show the caller's number are worth their weight in gold when it comes to these types of people. They most often are so wrapped up in themselves that they don't even stop to think that you have other people to serve as well. Often times they are just bored, with few friends, so they make a daily routine out of calling you every few hours.

If they persist, call them back later in the day and tell them that you are extremely busy delivering world-class service to a number of clients and that it will be much more efficient for both of you if they will call you as they feel they need to during the day and leave a message, but that you will review all of their messages at a certain time of the day and call them back with the answers to all of their questions at once. If they insist that their calls are very important and should be answered right away, just tell them that all of your clients' calls are important to you.

Interruptions can sometimes come from family members. The spouse calling about a hurt or sick child or some other high-priority emergency type of interruption. You should develop a go-to person on your team who can step in immediately to take over for you if this happens. They *"You should develop a go-to person on your team who can step in immediately to take over for you."* must be loyal beyond reproach and have an easygoing "hey, no problem" attitude toward life in general. They may have to suddenly excuse themselves from a meeting with another client to step in for you without notice. Be sure to find out what this person likes and reward him or her on a periodic basis just for being there for you.

Business Lunches (Make Them Count)

Let's face it; you've got to eat every day if you are going to maintain your health. Now, let's give credibility to the fact that at times you would like to use this time as a brief respite to a very, very busy day, which may extend well into the evening. Nothing is wrong with picking out your favorite place to eat, be it a fast-food place or a nice, quiet sushi bar and just sit there by yourself, relax, and collect your thoughts. However, don't forget that lunches can be highly useful ways to gain new information, create business relationships, and say, "Thank you," to your A group who is continually sending you referrals.

It is probably a good idea to set at least one or two lunch dates a week with these types of people in order to maximize and maintain relationships. Your A clients are probably the most important on-going source of new business that you will have, and they need to be shown special appreciation from time to time, so always allow a day or two a week to take one of them to lunch. A people hate to receive without giving back, so don't be surprised if, when you take one of them to lunch they have another referral for you. Learn to just accept it gratefully with a sincere, "Thank you." Also remember that they will want to talk about you. You want them to talk about them, so strike a balance so that you are both satisfied with the outcome.

If you decide that you want to become the go-to person for small custom home builders, start inviting them to lunch. Ask them about their business. What type of home do they usually build? What is their trademark, if any? Is there a part of town that they prefer over another? How can you help them to succeed and make more money? Do they have a broker with whom they work on a regular basis now, and can you compare your marketing plan to theirs?

Another very useful and highly productive type of lunch is where you schedule a regular day and time of the month in which several people from different businesses, who all rely somewhat on each other, meet and get to know each other. The goal being that as you get to know each other, you send each other referrals and keep it in the group. One admonition here, be *very* selective about whom you invite into this group. You could have a land developer, a builder, an insurance broker, a title company representative (who will often pick up the tab), a home inspector, a pool contractor, a roofer, an attorney, a venture capitalist, a landscape contractor, and the list goes on and on.

As you can see, all of these people could gain from knowing and using the services of the others from time to time. If you put the group together right, you can generate a lot of business from one another. Just be sure that each one knows the reason for the group—to become friends and to refer people to as needed.

Friends and Family Count Too

Building a highly successful and financially lucrative business is one of the most gratifying experiences that you can undertake, especially if you give part of your new-found wealth to charities and needy causes. It gives you an inner peace and glow that transcends the physical and soothes the soul. A word of caution though, I have done this for more than 30 years, *"You absolutely must take the time to include those who are close to you in your life as you travel this new road to wealth and financial freedom."* and I have seen many people come into the real estate business, do just as I have spelled out in this book, and end up divorced, estranged from their children, and without any real friends.

You absolutely *must* take the time to include those who are close to you in your life as you travel this new road to wealth and financial freedom. I don't mean to preach here; I just ask that you set a game plan in place that takes the important people in your life along this path with you instead of leaving them at the starting gate; you'll be running the great race and suddenly looking up and saying to yourself "What happened?

Money is easy to get. It is, at best, a barometer of how the financial aspect of your life is doing. Money, in itself, is not success. I know many, many people who have loads of money, and they are really shallow, lonely people who focused so hard on the money that everything else in their life turned into dust. Don't let that happen to you.

You will certainly make new friends along the way. You may also lose some friends along the way. If this happens, you need to assess what the friendship was really built on. A true friend really doesn't care if you are rich or poor, he or she just likes being around you. If this suddenly makes a difference, then you need to assess why. The reasons are many, and often the only way to find out what is wrong is to have a straightforward talk with them about it, and then let the relationship go where it's going to go.

Your parents and/or in-laws will almost certainly take on a different attitude about you. This can be positive or negative. I know from personal experience that an in-law who feels that he is king-of-the-hill in the family can be very upset at your new-found stature, and that person can subtly or not so subtly do things to sabotage you, so be careful about the family hierarchy as well.

10

Selling Your Business

Why Are You Selling? It Makes a Difference

Usually, when someone decides to sell a personal real estate business it is because they have climbed every mountain that they felt needed climbing. They have achieved a level of personal financial passive income through wise investments high enough to sustain themselves through their retirement years, and they have risen to whatever stature in the local and/or real estate community that they feel has chiseled their name permanently in the mystical stone of people to remember in the real estate business.

Sometimes people sell their personal real estate book of business for health, family relocation, or other reasons that are not entirely because they want to.

Your reason for selling will have much to do with why, how, and to whom you sell your business.

Get a Professional Appraisal

When you make the final decision to sell your business (and if you have followed the blueprint in this book for several years, you have created a saleable business), you will need a very accurate assessment of what it is worth. I can't stress enough the importance of getting a professional opinion of what your business is worth. If you go it alone and overprice it, you will do like a whole lot of sellers do and scare off any real prospects. You certainly don't want to under price it; you could easily end up leaving far more of your money on the table than the cost of the appraisal.

From a personal standpoint, when I left California for the Sonoran Desert of Arizona, I talked to two different agents there that had sold their businesses. One was a highly successful husband and wife team and one was an individual operator. They openly shared with me how they sold their businesses, and both really made sense from the buyer and the seller sides of the transaction. Since I worked as a team with my wife, Eileen, I took the best of each of the methods and combined them into a very rewarding sale of my "book," which is still paying me handsomely to this day, almost 5 years later.

I called national sales trainer Bill Barrett and asked him what he knew about formulas for selling a personal "book of business" (he called it the same thing), and I will include them in the formulas later in this chapter. He also gave me the name of Bob Bohlen, who is in Brighton, Michigan. Bob apparently evaluates the value of agents' personal businesses for a living and even negotiates the sale for a fee.

Is Your Partner or Team Buying You Out?

If you are not a sole operator and you have built a team, they, as a group, can be the best buyer for your business. They have already invested much time and effort into building it with you; they already know all or nearly all of the clients; and they already function as a group. Their only issue will be who steps up as the primary rainmaker.

The caution about going to this group is that you must do it in a way that does not panic them into thinking that your leaving is going to dismantle or otherwise negatively impact the team.

Whether you are selling to just one other person, a partner, or to your team, you can consider it an absolute must that you remain on with the team for several months while you, as a group, do some very effective and consistent advertising and marketing to the general public as well as the personal groups that you have developed as sources of business. You also should expect to be paid for this help with the transition in some fashion. All of this advertising and marketing must focus intensely on the fact that you have taken on a new partner or partners in your business. All advertising that you used to do that touted you as the owner of the business must now be converted to a "team theme," which tells all concerned that you now have an equal partner or partners.

After you have made the initial introduction of your new partners to your spheres of influence, you can become quite passive about any work that you do in direct connection with this transition. You should expect to be reasonably on call for the first 6 months or some other prenegotiated time period if one of the buyers needs you to lend your personal credibility to obtaining a listing or making a sale with one of your past customers or clients. This is best done via a prenegotiated referral fee each time that it is necessary.

If you are selling to someone besides your team, you will use the same "I" to "we" technique previously mentioned. You really can't expect anyone in their right mind to pay you a lot of money for a client base or book of business that is very loyal to you and doesn't know them at all. You will absolutely need to factor in a transition period—usually 4 to 6 months.

Cash or Paper?

All cash transactions for the purchase and sale of an agent's personal business are almost nonexistent. One of the main reasons is that your buyer or buyers usually don't have that kind of cash available, so here are some alternatives that I know are tested and have worked successfully.

If you are a one-person-show and are selling your book to another individual or group of individuals, get as much cash down payment as you can—I would say at least 20–30 percent—and negotiate a monthly payment that you can all live with for the remainder of the price. A 5-year term is common, including a negotiated interest rate, but if you have a huge business, you may want to adjust the time so that the payments are compatible with the amount of business generated after you are gone. Your buyer must sign a promissory note for the balance of the purchase price, and you should get a deed of trust against someone's real estate or some other enforceable method of collection if you can. Although personal notes are fully enforceable, attorney fees are always involved in the collection process, so be sure to have a clause in the unsecured note that says that they are fully liable for your attorney fees in the event of a default on their part, and spell out clearly what constitutes a default.

> "Do not even think of trying to draft the legal documents involved in the sale of your business."

Important note: Do not even think of trying to draft the legal documents involved in the sale of your business. Seek out the services of an attorney who specializes in contract issues.

Another method is to not establish a fixed price, but to get as much cash up front as you can and then receive referral fees on a sliding scale for every sale that is made involving one of your past clients for a predetermined period of time, which is usually 5–7 years. The amounts are totally negotiable but would usually start at 50 percent for the first year, 35 percent for the second year, 25 percent for the third year, 10 percent for the fourth year, and 5 percent for the fifth year. This is how I sold my business, except that I reserved the right to lifetime 25 percent referral fees for ten of my best clients. I received almost $20,000.00 in those referral fees last year alone.

Another method of sale is to take on a partner for a probationary period. After that period has passed and they are fully known to your clients, you are done. Get what cash you can up front, and they do *all* of the work (you are in the Bahamas or somewhere else just as nice after that). It is still your business, and, although they do the business, it is done in your name, and you pay them a referral fee on each transaction. The referral fee grows each year over a predetermined period until they are receiving 100 percent of the commission income. The downside to this method is that you are still connected both legally and reputation-wise, so you will need to evaluate your buyer very, very carefully if you use this method of sale.

Note: Remember, the reason that you bought this book was to stop selling real estate and to start to build a business. All businesses are built for an eventual sale, so take your time and do it right.

Deal from a Position of Strength

As mentioned before, a highly successful agent decides to sell his or her business for many different reasons; some good, some bad. In order to maximize the value of your business, you must never let on as to why you are selling—not to anyone!

"In order to maximize the value of your business, you must never let on as to why you are selling—not to anyone!"

As we have all found out through our experiences in helping other people negotiate the purchase and sale of real estate, the quest for monetary gain is an enormous factor in human nature. We've all seen it turn otherwise nice people into beasts.

The buyer or buyers of your business will surely be looking to negotiate the lowest price and best terms that they can get—that is just human nature. If you want to get the highest price and the best terms that you can get, you must be very tight-lipped about why you are selling, especially if it is because of some negative impact on your life that is forcing the sale, such as ill health or other factors. If health is the reason, don't wait too long, as you are probably going to start to show a physical decline at some point, and then it will be difficult to hide your reason for the sale. Sell when you think the time is the most opportune for you .You worked hard and took many an educated risk to get where you are, so negotiate early, do it with a poker face, and then sit back, relax, and enjoy the fruits of your labor.

11

2004 Income and Expense Statement

*T*he following Income and Expense Statement is based on the 2004 annual business plan developed in Chapter 8. Please review that plan as you look at these figures.

Marketing	$ 5,000.00	(magazines and other image-building media)
Newspaper advertising	$ 6,000.00	
Brochures	$ 2,000.00	(25 listings × 100 brochures × 78 cents each)
Direct mail items	$ 9,000.00	(items of value mailed to all groups)
Web site	$ 3,000.00	
Automobile	$ 8,000.00	(includes, payment, gas, maintenance, and tires)
Cell phone	$ 2,500.00	(includes long distance)
My salary	$ 79,300.00	(includes 10.1% additional for deductions)
Escrow administrator	$ 11,000.00	(4 months + 10.1% for deductions)
Licensed assistant(s)	$ 9,000.00	(bonus commissions + buyer referrals)
Buyer's representatives	$ –0–	(none hired in 2004)
Referral fees	$ 7,500.00	(paid to other agents at 25 percent of received)
Legal/accounting/E&O	$ 3,000.00	(includes LLC tax return preparation)
Dues/subscriptions	$ 1,000.00	(includes MLS, and so on)
Education	$ 1,000.00	
Client gifts	$ 2,400.00	
Cost of sale	$ 1,000.00	
Meals/entertainment	$ 4,000.00	(Includes A+ and out-of-town clients)
Office supplies	$ 2,000.00	
Postage/bulk mail	$ 3,000.00	
TOTAL EXPENSES	$159,700.00	

Income: (assumes $8,000,000 total sales at an average $250,000.00 price + 4 referrals)

22 personal sales or listings sold

$$\$250,000 \times 22 = \$5,500,000 \times 3\%$$
$$= \$165,000 \times 80\% \text{ commission split} = \$132,000$$

10 sales by your licensed assistant

$$\$250,000 \times 10 = \$2,500,000 \times 3\%$$
$$= \$75,000 \times 80\% = \$60,000 \times 60\% \text{ to you} = \$36,000$$

4 referrals received from brokers outside of the area

$$\$250,000 \times 4 = \$1,000,000 \times 3\%$$
$$= \$30,000 \times 80\% = \$24,000 \text{ to you.}$$

NET TOTALS:		
	Your personal sales	$132,000
	Licensed assistant	36,000
	Referral commissions	24,000
TOTAL INCOME TO YOU		$192,000
MINUS OPERATING EXPENSES		$159,700
NET PROFIT FROM		
YOUR BUSINESS		$32,300 (first year)

As you can see, by following this very realistic budget, you paid yourself a $72,000 salary, paid for your car, phone, and all other operating expenses, and made a $32,300 net profit. When comparing this to working on your own, don't forget to deduct your operating expenses like we did here.

I'll leave it to your imagination and your calculator to extrapolate what the total net income to you is after you hire the additional team members in the following years. Oh, by the way, don't forget that the facts and figures given here don't even start to talk about the value of vacations, long weekends, and every Sunday off. What's the dollar value of having that while your team is still out there taking care of business for you? Just sit back for a few moments, let your mind soar, and think about it. Then off to work you go!

12

Conversations with Mega-Producers

Interview with Nikki Mehalic—Long Realty Co., Tucson, Arizona
2002 sales volume was more than $30 million.

Bob Herd's comments are in bold and italicized type.
Nicki Mehalic's responses are in regular type.

Nikki, let's start with your background. Tell me a little about what you did prior to your real estate career.

Let's see, I was self-employed right out of college. I ran a screen printing business. I ran a mail order catalogue around the country. It was for college clubs and organizations. I started it at Arizona State University. It was cool because it taught me a lot about marketing and advertising. I put together an eight-page catalogue and bought mailing lists. It was great!

Well, that was for my T-shirts and then I bought a newspaper. It was an independently owned college newspaper, and I bought it to market my T-shirts. The readership targeted fraternities, sororities, and clubs, so I bought the paper as an advertising medium for my T-shirts. The advertising revenue from the newspaper netted about $10,000 an issue. I would give the clubs free ads if they would give me a year contract for all of their screen printing business, which was significant. I then sold both of those businesses. The long and short of it is that after that I didn't know what to do, so I worked for the American Heart Association doing fundraising.

While doing that, I met the developer of a Master Planned Community called Rancho Vistoso. He said to me, 'what are you doing working for a non-profit?' 'You should be in the for-profit world,' and he hired me as the Marketing Director for Rancho Vistoso. I learned all about development. I had a marketing background, and I learned all about development infrastructure and what went into the process of development such as roads, sewer, and water and working with the builders, what it took to create a planned unit development, builder's costs, and the different components of development.

My salary was $35,000 a year to do this job. It included going out to the real estate companies and asking them to come to Rancho Vistoso. After getting to know the real estate agents, I decided to become an agent and to specialize in Rancho Vistoso. It was considered the 'sticks' at the time. So, that's my background.

Q

So that's how you picked real estate. You started in development first, and then went into general brokerage. When did you start your real estate career?

In 1998.

Q

Tell me about your family. Tell me about your daughter.

Let's see, I remember taking the Tucson Realty & Trust Company's rookie training class when I was pregnant. I remember showing several lots the day before I gave birth, so pretty much right before my license went active was when I got pregnant. My first year, I was pretty much pregnant the whole time. My daughter, Lake, means everything to me. We have a lot of fun together.

Q

What do you do as a single mom to balance child care and a career like you've got?

Well, fortunately, I'm successful enough in my career that I can afford the best. So I have gotten very strict about my time with my daughter as far as not taking appointments in the evenings or on weekends. I have a gal that cleans my house, cooks dinner for us, and keeps my house in order so I don't have to deal with that when I'm at home with my daughter. But how do I balance it? It's hard. But I do. Like this weekend, Saturday and Sunday, they're all hers. So I refer a lot of business out. I give a lot of stuff away because it conflicts with my time with her.

That's great. OK, let's talk about your business. What has your sales volume been for the last three or four years?

Well it was $25 million last year, $19 million the year before, and $12 million the year before that.

And, you finished up 2002 with over $30 million?

Yes, I had a little over $30 million in sales this year.

About how many units does that represent per year?

I think last year it was 112.

Is that fairly common?

Yeah, uh-huh.

On average and given changing market conditions, how much is your sales volume going up each year?

I don't know, but 12-19-25. So that's 6 or 7 million a year. But in 2002, it only went up a little over five million because of the quiet conditions in the luxury market. Even with that I managed about a 25 percent increase over last year.

That's more than noteworthy, you know. How many hours a week did you work when you first started, and how many hours a week do you work now?

When I first started I probably worked 70 hours, 80 hours a week all the time, and now I probably work 60.

Q

That's a good balance. When you began your real estate career did you have a business plan, and if so, how has it evolved from then until now?''

Well I did in the sense that I knew that I started in October, and my first year I wanted to sell 1 million and I only had 3 months to do it, and I did it. My second year, which was my first full year, I had goals. I knew that I wanted to be a listing agent, and I don't know if I had a Number; I just knew that I had to get a lot of listings.

Q

Oftentimes a business plan won't have a definite number; it will just have direction. And yours seemed like, if I remember correctly, it seemed like it was very slanted toward being a strong listing agent.

Well that's what I learned, though... the most successful agents, what I saw, what I learned, what I heard, was that 'you had to list to exist.' I also found that working with buyers is just so draining and time consuming.

Q

That is can be—they're time consuming. It seems like you developed a plan early on to work with builders and developers.

Yes I did.

Q

Was that done intentionally?

Well, actually, I think it started out when I was a rookie. I had a good background in development so what I did was team up with a seasoned agent who knew a lot about land and who knew a lot about real estate and contract issues. With my marketing background, and my knowledge, and her expertise, we went after it together so it was very much intentional. I got our first subdivision, and I did the marketing presentation; I got the interview, and we did the pitch. I remember my partner looking at me and saying, 'We can do this!,' and

I looked at her, and I'm like 'No kidding! You know of course we can!' Then we went after four or five more subdivisions and got them all.

I remember; it was fun to watch!

It's exciting!

With the land becoming more of a scarce commodity here now, especially up in the northwest where you seem to specialize quite a bit, have you started evolving a plan to change your business plan to reflect that?

Absolutely, and I mean that's exactly what we've been doing.

Tell me a little bit more about it.

Eileen, Debbie, and I were talking about it. I was a land person and then the land dried up, so I evolved into this luxury and spec home specialist. I represented a lot of builders on specs when that was hot, then I was a luxury home agent when that whole market was hot. Well that market's gone so we've gone out there and done a lot of direct-mail campaigns for resale under $300,000. Right now I consider the bulk of my business is resale under $300,000. We've learned to adjust to changing market conditions, yet keep the image intact. People still perceive me as a luxury agent because they see those ads, but really the bread and butter is in our direct-mailing program directed at lower-priced homes. You know we just listed two today from direct mail. We just rock on direct mail, but it's because everybody already knows who we are, and they see our faces in all of our direct marketing pieces that we mail.

Yes, and you've built that reputation through a lot of very effective direct marketing.

So we're definitely involved in the current 'hot' market and we always will be, but once you've become a 'name' agent in a particular market segment, you need to maintain that as well because it will come and go with the economy and other factors. You don't want to start over each time a different market segment gets hot or cold. You simply have to budget to gain market share in one segment while maintaining in another.

But while you're doing that, you're still maintaining at a lower key, you're still maintaining your presence in the luxury market, right?

Certainly! Three months ago lots were hot. Then we had a couple $600,000 spec homes sell, and then this last month it's been lots under $300,000. So, if we were in just one market segment we'd be broke right now.

Yeah, that's right. I've talked to some other high-production agents recently that said that they've done the same thing. That they used to do strictly luxury properties and nothing else, but with the shift in the economy they're not anymore, they just stopped. I think that you are smart to maintain some continuity in that market because it will rebound at some point, and you will have an immediate and lucrative market share.

You can't afford to overdo it because it costs money, but you need to maintain a presence. At the same time you look forward to those $300,000 houses. Those are nice checks and pay the bills while the luxury market is quiet.

Yes they are. About what percentage of your business is listing versus sales?

Eighty percent is listings.

Eighty percent listings and 20 percent sales?

Eighty percent or higher.

We'll talk more about teams later on, but you refer a lot of your buyers to your team, right?

Correct. Unless they're a direct relationship from a referral or from a close client of mine, I make every attempt to assist them, but a lot of times I don't even have time for that. I refer most of my buyers to my buyer's reps.

Q *About what percentage of your business comes from the following sources?*

Q *Referrals:*

Twenty-five percent.

Q *About 25 percent from referrals? Okay. How much from marketing, in other words, magazines and other image-building media, not advertising.*

Maybe 5 or 10 percent.

Q *Five to ten percent. And, is that mainly high-end customers and clients, or is it across the board?*

You know, it might even be less, Bob, because I think that all of those image pieces are just that, they're public relations to get to know me. They burn who I am into somebody's mind. So, usually they receive something from me, and it triggers a thought process like, 'oh yeah, we've seen her; we feel like we know her, let's call her.' I don't know how many people call me from a marketing piece and want me to list. Usually...maybe it's 5 percent or lower.

Q *About how much from advertising? Things like realtor.com, other Web sites, newspapers, homes for sale type magazines, and that sort of thing?*

Not direct mail?

Q *No, not direct mail; just ads showing homes for sale in some media.*

Maybe 10 percent.

> **Q**
>
> *Ok. You don't have a telemarketer that cold-calls for you, right?*

No.

> **Q**
>
> *How much of your business comes from direct mailing?*

Wait, how many people have telemarketers?

> **Q**
>
> *Nobody I've interviewed so far. Some do, though. Curt Stinson cold-calls almost every day, and he had 106 closings last year.*

Direct mail accounts for 50 percent or more of my listings.

> **Q**
>
> *That's effective mailing, let me tell you.*

It's always the same place.

> **Q**
>
> *Tell me about your marketing and advertising program. What do you do, and how do you do it?*

We have a system that we've put into place, and it's actually... we're fine-tuning it all the time to make it better. It's so cool. We get a listing; we have a template for flyers; the template gets filled out; it's faxed or e-mailed to our printer; then our printer works it up and e-mails it back; then we proof. I send it back, and it goes out to every active agent; then the pictures are uploaded to MLS and the newspaper. We fax the ad forms. So, it's all been based on systems; we have a 20-item checklist.

When I take a listing, here's what happens: It's pretty much Debbie and I who do that. Eileen does the logistical part, the paperwork. But, we have a system; the system has been... we are always working on it. I always joke with Debbie, 'How can we be leaner?' 'How can we be more efficient?' And, we get all these calls after we get a listing. So now Debbie and I are working on a form that would give the people the opportunity to write their own comments for ads and the MLS. Then it's one less phone call we have to field after we take a listing. So we're always coming up with stuff to make it more efficient.

Q

So you've got a highly systemized operation then?

Very systemized, and it's the same marketing program for every person unless they want to deviate, and I never say no to anybody as far as 'I want to be in the magazine'—no problem, it's all self-promotion.

Q

What percentage of your gross commission income do you allocate in your business plan for marketing, and how do you track its effectiveness?

For the most part, I ask them 'how did you hear about me,' and they tell me things like 'I see you everywhere, I got this in the mail, I feel like I know you.' So that's how I track it, by asking people when they call me.

Q

About what percent of your gross commission income do you allocate for advertising and marketing?

It's probably about 15 to 20 percent.

Q

Well, that falls right in line with what Russell Long told me. He said 18 percent, too. Around 15 percent to 18 percent, that's a theme that I've seen carry through all of you, and you're right on track there.
Can you supply me with copies of you marketing and advertising pieces?

Oh yeah. Do you want my templates too? Those are great.

Q

Give me some of your finished product, because what I'm going to do is actually get them down to book size and include them as marketing pieces in the back.

Right, I should give you the templates because those would be good for people.

Q

Good idea. What programs or methods do you have in place to retain past clients and receive referrals from past clients?

We're doing monthly mailing to our sphere of influence. Basically a modified Brian Buffini program.

Q

A modified 100 percent type referral program?

Right.

Q

And what do you do? Do you follow it up with phone calls, or is it strictly mailings?

Right now it's strictly mailings.

Q

If you made about 20 phone calls a month to those people, what do you think it would do to your business?

Huge! Debbie said five a day, Nikki, I want you to call five people a day. I told her to put five a day on my desk, because I don't think I would do it otherwise.

Q

I don't think 5 would work for you with what you've got going on, but you could do 20 a month to start.

I can't even call back all of my current clients. You know, the people that leave me messages every day.

Q

About how many people do you have in your database?

Maybe about 300 right now.

Q

OK. And do you contact the people in your database regularly, and does it vary in accordance with the relationship that you have with them?

We do have them categorized A, B, C, but right now because it's so few, we do all of them the same.

And you do them more than monthly don't you?

Well, I do my monthly thing where I send them something of value, but most of my clients are in my neighborhood and where I sell, so they're always getting my just listed just sold post cards.

So you use the just listed/just sold thing as a regular form of contacting them along with a special mailing just to them?

Yes, and then, like last year, I sent everyone in Rancho Vistoso tickets to the Greek Festival, and then I sent everybody my open house extravaganza—14,000 invitations in Oro Valley and so I do crazy stuff like that—but it keeps my name in front of them, and they all remember me.

Yes they do. Yes they do!

And even Eileen has become a little bit of a celebrity!

How about your team? Tell me about your team and how it works?

Well, thanks to you, when I was doing my second year, maybe going on my third year when I hit $12 million, you said, 'You're at a point where you need to hire an assistant.' And, I was really scared, but I did it, and the next year I did $7 million more. So it was huge, and it was working; I worked less. So what has evolved now is that I hired the first assistant, and she manages escrows and all the paperwork and fields most of the calls to the office during the day, which is huge as it frees me up to be out in the field, actually I consider myself as the business development specialist.

The rainmaker.

That's all I do. I was thinking about my job description and I am, yeah I'm always business development because I'm always out getting new listings more than I'm selling.

Q *That's the way it's supposed to work.*

So, I'm business development and negotiations. That's what I do. When I do my listing presentation, I say that I'm an advertising agency and a negotiator. That's what I do, so hiring Eileen got me to be out in the field doing way more business development.

Q *So Eileen's the office manager?*

Office manager, she runs the show. I mean I don't even know what's going on with the escrows half the time.

Q *With competent help like her, you shouldn't have to. What does she do? Give me a brief description.*

What doesn't she do? Umm, all the paperwork to puts the listing together, all of the paperwork for handling the escrows...

Q *So complete escrow file management. Does she set appointments for you, for inspectors, and things like that?*

Yes. She sets all the appointments, termite inspectors, works with the other agents on the other side of the transaction, I mean, she pretty much does 100 percent when I hand her the file. When we make a sale, she takes it from there.

Then I hired a second assistant about two years ago. I don't call her an assistant; she's my marketing director, because we have so many listings that I couldn't handle writing all the ads, ordering the virtual tours, and the photographs, etc. She gets paid a salary plus she gets first crack at many of my buyers. Debbie is my marketing and advertising person. She does all the advertising, puts together all the brochures, and she's very computer savvy; she manages the Brian Buffini referral system. She also set up the system for when we take a listing. She put the whole process on a form and made it easier to fax and e-mail, and it's more comprehensive and easier to use.

Your office manager works what, a 40—45 hour week or there-abouts? What about the marketing manager, how many hours a week does she work? What's your relationship with her, and how does she work? Is she an independent contractor an employee?

She gets a monthly stipend of $2,000, and then she gets perks, like at the Honeybee subdivision, she gets a half-point on every sale and the first crack at many of my buyers, and she pays me a referral fee of 30 percent, so she'll get most of the commission, for the most part.

Do you have a telemarketer or any other team members?

No, anything else I do, I like, sub-out. If I have a mailing, and we're all too buried, then we'll pay someone hourly or, I just hired a new girl to go around to my listings once a week and make sure they're all looking their best. In other words, she sees that the toilets are flushed and the weeds are pulled; the flyer boxes are full; the sign-in sheets are there; and things like that.

Let's talk a little bit about company support. How much office space do you and your team occupy—either square feet or number of desks?

We have three desks in two offices and maybe 300 square feet.

What benefits does your company provide to you and your staff— by that I mean extra advertising or supplies or company paid staff help, accounting services for your team, special marketing incentives, or any-thing like that? Is there anything that's not being provided that should be in your opinion?

Just my office space, I don't think I get any other perks. What do they bring to the table? The things that Long Realty brings to the table for me are name recognition, market share, and great advertising programs.

The Homebuyer's Guide and the Internet site and the subsidized newspaper advertising.

> **What has their Internet site meant to you?**

Not much.

> **You have your own, right?**

I link my name to their site, but, for as many hits as they get a month, I sure don't see them, and I've got market share in Oro Valley, so I always wonder where those leads are really going.

> **The amount of hits is incredible; it's in the millions per month, but that includes agents going on-line checking e-mails and stuff like that, too. There are a lot of inquiries, but anything that goes directly to the company Web site, they send to the office that's closest to the property that the inquiry was on, and then how the office disseminates it is up to the individual manager.**

So my listing goes to my office; it doesn't go right to me.

> **If it goes to your Web site, then it goes right to you. But if it goes to the company Web site, the company makes a decision about which office should get the lead and then the manager decides who gets it from there.**

OK, that sounds fair.

> **Is there anything that's not being provided to you right now that you think should be in your opinion?**

Yes. One of the things that I talked to Steve, the CEO, about was when we buy a virtual tour it's on Long's Web site, but it doesn't go over to Realtor.com, so I have to pay to put it on there, too. It would be great if it was automatically rolled over.

Q

Hmm. That's a good point; what does that cost?

Debbie orders them; I don't know. It's just one more thing that I was going to look into because it's free to the agents in our company. Because everything's downloaded they just haven't figured out how to do it yet, but it would be a big money saver for the agents if they figure it out.

Q

Depending on a couple of things, producing the very high sales volume that you produce every year clearly sets you apart from the average real estate agent. What do you do that it so effective and different from them?

Well, with the volume that I do, I am in real estate. I am in the game every day.

Q

That's a winning philosophy if I've ever heard one.

I'm not part-time; I love it. I live it; I breathe it. I find out everything I can; I learn whatever I can. Even when I'm in somebody's house because I'm out to dinner I'm looking at what kind of window casings they have, what kind of cabinets are those? How much was this flooring as an upgrade? You know, I'm always learning.

Q

It would seem to me that your constant attention to your market plan would have something to do with that. I mean how you constantly upgrade and shift it. Would you agree with that?

Absolutely. That's what I always say to the girls. We don't have any business? Send out another mailer. That's how we get calls.

Q

In your opinion, what's the single biggest benefit that you bring to your clients? What kind of knowledge?

Well, I know real estate in Oro Valley. Nobody can match me. I made it a point to know it and learn it, to know the developers, know the land costs, construction costs, know finishes. Like I said, I know my business in Oro Valley. I don't know it outside of Oro Valley so I get nervous. But I am very confident and cocky, and then I provide excellent customer service.

> **So, like the other mega-producers that I've interviewed, you go narrow and deep, right?**

Yes, I really believe in that.

> **That's a great point. Tell me where you see the residential real estate agent's role in the home-buying process going in the next several years?**

I think the Internet exposing people to more information is going to make our role as counselor even more important. And, they're going to turn to us, now they have access to the information, and they want to turn to the experts and say 'Am I interpreting this right?' 'Can you hold my hand through the process?' I think its going to almost make us more interactive, touchy-feely with our clients as opposed to people thinking it's going to take our business away. So we're empowering them with information, but they don't know exactly what to do with it or what it really means, so they need to interact with us.

> **Do you see the market kind of evolving to fewer and fewer agents doing more and more business?**

Absolutely. I already kind of feel like it is that way. That's part of my listing presentation, is that 90 percent of the business is done by 10 percent of the agents. I say I'm in the game every day, I'm not that 90 percent, I'm 10 percent, and I'm number one in Oro Valley. Then they think about who they have. At an interview yesterday I was the third agent, and they called me 10 minutes afterwards, 'It's yours.' It was Oro Valley, and I was in the zone.

> **You were in your element there that's for sure.**

I think that agents that aren't very knowledgeable are going to go by the wayside.

Do you see an increasing importance of our negotiating skills over what they used to be on behalf of our clients?

Absolutely! It's so funny that you asked me that; I mean, maybe it was a lead-in question, but for the last two months, my listing presentation has emphasized marketing and negotiation. When you hire me, I'm your negotiator. I did 112 transactions last year. I'm in the game. I know what I'm doing because I do so many negotiations, and I'm getting to the point that for the last four months, when I have been negotiating, I knew what they were going to say before they said it, and I knew what was going to happen, but it took me five years. My managers always knew what they were going to say and do next, but I could never see that, and now I can see it, and I can hear it, and now I feel like I am a good negotiator. That really creates confidence. It was this revelation that I had. I was like yeah! I knew what they were going to say. I played the card right.

What are the top three pieces of advice that you can give to a real estate agent that wants to become a mega-producer.?

Come up with a business plan and stick to it. I think that you should know what you are doing. Learn the market. Learn, I mean there's a lot of it that has to do with personality too, but if you're knowledgeable and people know that you're knowledgeable, then they trust you and you build this automatic rapport. For the business plan, know your business and have total dedication to your craft.

Anything else you'd like to tell a person reading this book?

Yes. Never ever compromise what's right. If I ever get in a situation that's gray, I always back off. Never compromise yourself and your beliefs, then you'll always be able to sleep at night.

Interview with Russell Long—Long Realty, Tucson, Arizona
2002 sales volume was more than $41 million.

Bob Herd's comments are in bold and italicized type.
Russell Long's reponses are in regular type.

> **Russell, tell me a little bit about your background; what did you do prior to your real estate career?**

I grew up in Tucson; I graduated from high school in 1967. Went to the university, was on the 6-year plan there because I switched colleges and did a stint with Uncle Sam, and after graduating in 1973, I became a high school teacher. I was an English and speech teacher, and I was the speech and debate coach before I got into real estate. My 5-year teaching contract as a tenured teacher was for $12,500. My wife was a teacher, and we wanted to start a family. We knew if she quit teaching, we could not afford it on 'twelve five.' As a matter of fact, it was below the poverty level at that time for a family. We decided that she would teach for 1 more year and let me get started in real estate. We did that, and my first year in real estate, I made $25,000.

> **And that was what year?**

1977-78. We made $25,000 as compared to the twelve-five I would have made as a teacher, and we thought we were rich. And, it's been a great career, so I started in 1977.

> **And your entire career has been here in Tucson?**

Yes, all with Long Realty.

> **It was your grandfather who started the firm, right?**

Yes, my grandfather started the company, and he retired in 1952 and gave my dad the business for $1.00. There wasn't much, it was one office and eight sales people. My dad took over in 1952 and he's really the guy who built it into the large corporation. By the time he retired in 1980, there were ten offices and several hundred sales people.

Q

It's really grown! Tell me a little about your family.

My wife, Christy, is my partner. She almost totally does advertising— that's her role in our business. I estimate that she brings in about half our business.

Q

That much?

Yes, because of the advertising, and because of the people she knows in Tucson; you know, lots of them will list with us because they know Christy.

Q

OK, it makes sense.

I have a daughter, Jennifer, who's 24, who just graduated from New York University. She's in musical theater, and she is there now trying to get on stage. And, then I have a daughter who's 21 who just graduated from beauty school, and she wants to be a rock and roll star; she's very, very talented.

She has a manager and a producer, and she is very serious. She's recorded two 'demo' CDs, and she's under new management getting ready to do a third demo CD, and from that they're going to try and get her a recording contract. She's good. So that's it, my wife and two kids.

Q

And your mom works with you too, right?

My mom works with us full-time. She's 78 years old and works full-time.

Q

Yeah, she's very energetic; just an incredible lady.

She loves it, and she hates weekends because by the end of the weekend she's ready to come back to work. She hates being alone, and we all get along really well.

She's been around realtors too much of her life.

I guess.

We'll get into what her functions are a little bit later. Tell me about your business now. What has your sales volume been for the last three or four years, just approximately?

Well, this year, I think that I will close more than $40 million worth of sales. Last year was our worst year, actually, and I think we did about $24 million through the Multiple Listing Service. Last year, was a combination of me losing focus and thinking about moving over here from the central office was a distraction, and then, of course, the stock market problems really hurt the upper-end market that I work so heavily. Then September 11 put the kibosh on things, so last year, we just did $24 million, but the year before we did $33 million. 2002 was the best year we've ever had. Typically, we've been doing 60 to 95 units a year. Right now, I think we have our highest average sales price ever, which is about $450,000.

That's high for Tucson, too. For an average sales price, that's way up there.

I think typically we've been around the $350,000 to $400,000 range, something like that.

You just closed on a $2 million listing of yours that sold, if I remember, right?

That's right.

Larry Sawyer sold it here, in-house, right?

Correct, that's correct.

Your sales volume, except for a 1-year dip, seems to be fairly steady, but 2002 was significantly higher.

Well, significantly higher than last year. But we're sort of back on track, and I'm sort of back on focus. I would estimate that our sales volume has been going up a minimum of 10 percent a year.

That's healthy. How many hours a week did you work when you first got into the business, and about how many hours a week do you work now?

I don't think that I work any more or less hours now than I did then. I probably work pretty much the same hours.

So you kind of set a pattern and stuck with it.

Yes, I work roughly, 70 to 80 hours a week. I'm in the office between 6:30 and 7 in the morning and get home between 6 and 7 at night 5 days a week. Weekends, I'll try to take a little bit of each morning off, but typically I'll be to work Saturday and Sunday anywhere from 11 to 2. So I'll work between two-thirds of the day to half a day on weekends. Sometimes, I work all day long if I'm really busy, and sometimes I'll work another 8 or 12-hour day. I don't like doing that, and I don't really consider myself a workaholic. Maybe I'm delusional.

Well, when you love what you do then it's a little easier than when you don't.

Well, it's not so much loving what I do, because I do like to goof-off, and I have a lot of hobbies, and I like doing outdoor stuff, but when the business is there and people expect you to get the work done and they're counting on you, I go do the work.

That's the philosophy that wins. When you began your real estate career did you have a business plan; and if you did, how has it evolved over the years?

Oh, yes! I had a very specific business plan, and it was a program that I had set up for my agents when I was in management. I had one goal, and the goal was the number of listing presentations that I would do in a year.

Interesting.

I had them broken down to a per-week basis and then based upon the number of listing presentations that I did I had that broken down to a percentage of listings that I would get, percentage of listings that would sell, and the volume that would produce. So my goal was not a dollar volume goal or a sales volume goal, it was simply how many listing presentations could I get? I don't remember what the numbers were, but I followed that pretty religiously for about 5 or 6 years, and I tracked every listing that I got, what it led to, what volume that created, and interestingly enough it came out to be that year-in, year-out, for every dollar I listed there would be a dollar in sales. So if I listed a million dollars worth of property then I would have $750,000 in listings sold and $250,000 in sales. So, not every listing I would have would sell, but probably 75 percent of them would and then from that inventory I would make up the balance of my business, another 25 percent, in sales, and I still estimate that that's what I do today. Probably 75 percent in listings sold and 25 percent in sales, and much of the 25 percent in sales is because of my listing inventory.

OK, that makes perfect sense.

Regarding how the plan has evolved, I followed that plan for 5 or 6 years, and then I just kind of lost interest in the plan, and it just seemed to me that business was happening, and it was going to happen, and I quit using the plan, and I just work as hard as I can.

So your business has evolved now to where the great majority of your business is coming from referrals from satisfied customers and repeat customers instead of the other type of thing. That's good information. Do you work a specialty or niche market, and if you do, can you describe to me what it is and how you evolved into working it? For example, you work the luxury market a lot, you're a very dominant force in the luxury market in Tucson. Was that on purpose as a designed plan, or did it evolve out of something?

It sort of evolved to that, and I think that we evolved into that. I remember when we started, part of my plan was to work expired listings and to work anything at $150,000 and above, and so, you know I was definitely going after a lower market, but my wife, who has an art degree, placed some really great ads in some of the glossy magazines, and we started getting some phone calls off of the ads. Then we get some upper-end listings through a lot of marketing on the upper-end listings and that sort of snowballed into what we do today.

As I said, we had an average sales price last year of about $450,000, but we go all ends of the market. I just had a sale last week for $99,000, and then we got some really big ones, but I like doing little ones, too. I like being a full-service realtor. If somebody just calls me off the street who has a $99,000 house, I'll probably refer it to someone else, but the guy whose house we sold last week was represented by my dad when he bought the house in 1965, and my grandfather had done the financing on it for him, so you don't want to turn that stuff down. They're an elderly couple. I met their granddaughter, who said next time she did real estate business she would do it with us. So you do a $99,000 sale, and you meet the granddaughter who buys a $400,000 house from you—that's what full service is all about.

Exactly. From the time Christy started placing the ads that started getting you the high-end buyers, about how long did it take for you to evolve into doing mostly high-end properties like you do now?

Surprisingly, it really didn't take very long. Because when you've got some upper end properties, and you do the marketing that you need to do on those homes, the word gets out that you're doing it. Fortunately I'm blessed with a name that helps me get some phone calls, and people would see my name, and they'd see us advertising an expensive piece of property; they didn't know a real estate agent, and they'd call us.

That makes sense. Just to reconfirm, what percentage of your business comes from listings?

Well, probably 75 percent listings and 25 percent sales, and as I said the 25 percent on the selling side much of that comes off of our inventory. I pick those buyers up off of our inventory. That one sale I had this year for 1.8 million came off of a sign call. That would never have happened if I hadn't had the listing.

Q *Tell me approximately what percentage of your business comes from the following sources.*
Referrals.

I know this is going to sound really low, but I'm guessing about 40 percent comes from referrals. I went to lunch with Robin (Robin-Sue Kaiserman was the number-one agent in Tucson for nine straight years) a few weeks ago, and she made an interesting comment to me; she said, 'You know, I don't think I'm ever going to get out of real estate 101; I still do all the basics and when am I not going to have to do the basics?' She said, 'I still do mass mailings, and I still deliver to my sphere to influence.' So what she was telling me was that you never completely leave the basics, and I piped in and I said, 'I agree with you completely.' I hear these real estate agents say that they're 100 percent referral business. That's a bunch of garbage. I'm around 40 percent, and 20 percent magazines, maybe 20 percent from other advertising.

Q *How useful has the Web site been to you?*

Fabulous, absolutely fabulous! We had four sales the first half of last year that I can attribute to the Virtual Reality alone. One of them was a Long Realty agent out of the Tanque Verde office. Her client used the Virtual Reality program on our Web site and called her up and said, 'Call my aunt here in Tucson. I want my aunt to see the house.' The aunt saw it, called them, and said, 'It's a great house.' They made an offer on it, site unseen, just based on the Virtual Reality, subject to their approval of the inspection of the property.

Q *What price range was that?*

$250,000. We had the identical situation with a $1,025,000 home. Sherry Medina in this office sold my listing in Ventana. Same identical scenario except there was no aunt involved. They already knew Ventana. I think they were in California. They knew Ventana, and they knew the street, and so from the Virtual Reality, they saw what they liked, signed a contract site unseen, subject to approval of the property and the inspections and closed escrow. So, the Internet and the Virtual Reality have been very, very helpful this year.

It's an effective and growing phenomenon, that's for sure. Do you do any telemarketing at all, any cold-calling, or anything like that?

Cold-calling? No. No we don't.

Did you do it when you first started?

I did some, but I hated it.

Yeah, most people do. I used to do a lot of it my first three or four years in the business, but by then so much of my business was coming by referral that I didn't have to do it any more.

When I got started back in sales we did open houses, we worked a farm, we farmed Skyline Bel air. We still farm Skyline Bell air. And, we worked a sphere of influence, and we advertised. So, between open houses, sphere of influence, farming, and we did mass mailings, and we still do. Lots of mailings.

Are the mass mailings to various areas where you've got a listing and you let people know about it or is there one particular area?

Every single listing we take we mail to the immediate neighbors. When we make a sale we mail to the immediate neighbors. Sometimes we mail to a broader range. Right now one of the main things that we do is work our sphere of influence, and we send them a quarterly piece.

We just talked about a little bit of it, but would you describe your marketing and advertising program in greater detail for me.

I sort of wrote it down here. We get a lot of calls off of *Homes & Land* magazine and so we take two pages in *Homes & Land,* and we take two pages in every issue. The reason we go in *Homes & Land* is that it's all color; it looks good; and it's nationally known. People who come here from Boston; they get off the airplane at the airport; and they walk by that rack of real estate magazines; and they have *Homes & Land* in Boston so they see *Homes & Land,* and they're familiar with it, and they grab it. Additionally, when we advertise in *Homes & Land,* then our property gets put on their Internet site. So every house in here is on www.homesand-land.com. We get an awful lot of business from this magazine.

We also do a lot of advertising in the *Home Buyer's Guide* (a Long Realty magazine), and two of the benefits that we have are that we do lots of front covers. Because this is the latest one, and this is our house on the front cover, so that's some of the advertising we do.

> ***Does the front cover tend to generate more calls than inside? It's so highly visible that it seems to create an image of what you guys do.***

You sent Mary Byczek up to talk to me, and I told her that the main reason that I advertise now, and the main reason that I hold open houses is to get listings. I don't hold open houses to pick up buyers, that's a side benefit. My main reason for advertising, for holding open houses, is I want to meet the people who are considering selling, and they will often go around to see what the competition is. So many, many listings we get because the clients like this kind of thing.

> ***What are some of the other things you do?***

Well, aside from this front cover we generally take a page or two on the inside, and then we buy extra slots, and these help sell properties. I get lots of calls from real estate agents from other companies whose buyers pick these magazines up. They say 'can you give me the MLS number on this property?' and, because I carry my inventory with me I just pull it out and give them the MLS number. We do a lot of advertising in the Long section of the newspaper.

My opinion is that picture classified ads in our Sunday newspaper sec-tion are the best advertising you can do. If we put one of these picture ads in and do it in conjunction with the regular open house ad, we will get three or four times as many people to the open house than if we just put it in the regular open house section.

Do you put it both?

Absolutely, always in both. So any of these that are over here in the picture section that are open houses are also going to be back here in the regular open house section. Every house that we hold open is on the Internet.

Have you been able to track very well whether when people come to the open house are they coming in off the Internet ad or off of this ad?

I don't do the open houses. I get other agents to do it, so I don't know. I do know that the open house works or that the Web site works for open houses because for example I had one cancel in Hacienda Del Sol Estates last week, and I canceled the ad, but I forgot to take it off the Web site, and a guy showed up who may just end up buying it. So I know that people do go out for those.

Yes, they do. My feedback, as the branch manager here, is that more and more people are coming in directly from the Internet posting of the open house.

We advertise in *Tucson Lifestyle* (an upscale Tucson magazine), and we'll generally take a page. We also generally take a page in *Tucson Guide Magazine*.

This Tucson Lifestyle magazine is not a real estate magazine; this is more about Tucson, and there are several real estate ads in here. What kind of calls does this generate to you?

High-end calls; not very many calls, but good ones. Quality calls, particularly in fall and the winter when the out-of-town people are here and looking to buy or sell property.

Q

So this would be most effective during the high season?

That's right, and then the same thing with *Tucson Guide*; we advertise a full page in *Tucson Guide,* and we do *Tucson Guide* because it goes in the hotel rooms and all of the resorts. So it's in La Paloma, Ventana, the Sheraton, *Westward Look*, the same kind of magazine as this, and we do a full page in there. We take generally a half to a full-page in the *Desert Leaf magazine* as well.

Q

The Desert Leaf is kind of a neighborhood type of newspaper?

Foothills and Tanque Verde school districts. So it's all across the Foothills out across to the northeast.

Q

How often does it come out?

It comes out once a month, and we advertise generally every Foothills home that we have; we get a lot of calls off of this also. Once again, Bob, the reason that we're advertising is we're advertising because people considering selling their homes will often see who does the most advertising. They are asking themselves 'who's going to market my property the most.' So that's why we get probably 40 to 50 percent of our business off of our advertising and marketing.

Q

Are there any other advertising media that you use?

Well, yes; we advertise on the Internet. We do a virtual reality, and we'll physically have five to eight additional photos of each property.

Q

Do you have a bottom-end price point where you don't do the virtual reality?

I do the virtual reality on every single house.

Q

Regardless of price range?

That's right, I'd say that for every property priced at $200,000 and above, we'll do one of these brochures.

I've seen many of your color brochures with several pictures of the property; they're really nice. I'm going to include a sample in another chapter if you don't mind.

No, that would be fine. Then we hire 'Floor Plans First' to do the floor plans for every house that we do, including that $99,000 one we did last week. One of the reasons I hire 'Floor Plans First' to do that is that they will often come up with more square footage than the assessor has and that helps us get higher prices for our clients. On that little house last week, it was 832 square feet according to the assessor. 'Floor Plans First' came up with 855 square feet. He's made several sales for me because he's shown more square footage than what the assessor came up with.

And that basically helps from a liability as well as a marketing standpoint.

That's right. And he puts these online, so we have them in the house, they're online, and of course the seller loves these things.

Does he do the property brochures that go on the for sale sign out front?

No, I used to do those when I first got started, but I found them to be a real pain because when I'm driving down the street, and I see one of those things, and I get out to get the flyer, and they're gone, then I think that the agent is negligent, and so then what I did is I started to have the seller stuff them. I'd give the seller a whole stack and say, 'Make sure there's just ten in there every day. Then I found that I did-n't get very many phone calls off of my properties. When the buyers picked up a flyer, they got every bit of information that they wanted, and I did not have an opportunity to tell them about the house I had right around the corner. If they had called me, and it turned out to be too much money for them, I've got one right around the corner, and it's $100,000 less. Why don't you go see that? I quit using those things;

I don't use them at all, I get far more calls on my signs, and if the seller wants one of those then I'll put one on. But I always explain to the seller the advantages and disadvantages.

Q *OK, interesting point. That's worth thinking about because it saves you a lot of money and gets you more business, right?*

Exactly! Now, just a couple of other things that I wrote down. We do some real expensive advertising too, for example, we placed a big ad in the 'City of Arizona's' program for the arts publication. The Community Center does an artist series; we put a big ad in that.

Q *That's more of an image-building type of marketing piece, but it would surely lead to some direct business as well.*

Q *About what percentage of your gross commission income do you allocate in your business plan for marketing and advertising, and how do you track its effectiveness?*

Well, I would say probably one of the areas where we don't do very well is in tracking that kind of thing.

Q *That's an all-to-common issue in our industry.*

I don't really track it, and we just keep advertising until the home sells. But part of the beauty in that we almost never get turned down for a listing extension because they know how much money we have spent. They see that we're doing open houses as often as we can, either ourselves or through other agents holding them open, and we make a point of sending our clients a copy of every ad that we run.

Q *That is so important!*

And frankly, Bob, most of our sellers are spoiled; they really are. They don't know what they are getting. I mean they have no clue. They haven't sold a house for 10 years, they think that everyone does what we do. This past year we spent for all advertising, I can't remember what it was... somewhere between $175,000 and $200,000, and we just keep spending until that thing sells. But in the end, we make a very good profit.

If you're talking about a sales volume that is in excess of $41 million, you're looking at over a million dollars in gross commission income, so you'd be spending about 18 percent to 20 percent of your gross income on advertising and marketing, and that's really right in line with nearly everyone else that I have interviewed. It's working on a higher plane, and that's kind of what the essence of this business is about. So that's good information.

What programs or methods do you have to retain past clients and receive referrals from them?

Well, that's another thing that we probably don't do as well on as we should. Christy has a mailing program in her computer at home, and the principal thing that we do is send them a quarterly mailing.

To all of your past clients in your database?

Everybody. We update the database; I use a Palm Pilot. I have my whole database in the Palm Pilot. I update the Palm Pilot daily at home so that it's in the computer as well. Christy goes to my Palm Pilot information and synchs it into her program, and then she does seasonal things like that.

Like these basketball schedule mailers and...

Keeper cards. They're all keeper cards, and we do four of those a year; then we mail a holiday card to our entire sphere of influence, and we mail a calendar. So they're getting something from us four to six times a year.

That's very effective client contact.

And I don't make any phone calls to them, but they are receiving things from me. Christy has all of our real upper-end clients on either the 'Tucson Lifestyle' or 'Tucson Guide' mailing list, and they all get a *Tucson Guide* or *Tucson Lifestyle* magazine that says on it that it's courtesy of us. And, we get lots of phone calls thanking us for them, and it didn't cost us anything.

> ### *That's a good program, especially if it's free.*

I'm guessing we probably have maybe 400 names in our database who are people we continue to mail to who did not move out of town. If they move back to New England, then we just don't mail to them too much.

> ### *How often do you synch this and update it?*

Several times a year. Christy is always kind of working on it, and when we need extra help, she has a college girl who works for her who does a lot of stuff for us, and that's one of the things the girl does is synch my Palm Pilot with Christy's database.

> ### *She does this so often to be sure that the information is current, right?*

That's right; it's very important that it's totally current.

> ### *And do the mailings vary according to the relationship you have with them?*

Well, as I said, pretty much all of them are getting four to six mailing pieces a year, but because we both grew up in Tucson, a lot of them are family and friends, and so we'll see them at social functions, you know. I mean we may see some of our clients 15, 20, 30, times a year. We sold a woman's house last year and sold her another lot. We see her probably 50 times a year, maybe once a week.

> ### *Your team consists of you, and your mom, and Christy, and a part-timer?*

Well, Christy does all of our advertising, she really does not sell at all. I think I told you the other day that she sold one home in the last four years. I told her that I told you that, and she said, 'I sold three houses!' But she does not show property unless it's an emergency.

Basically all of the property showing and listing appointments are taken care of by you personally, right?

My mother or me. My mother is licensed, and I do all of the showing. If our listings are being shown, and somebody has to be there, either my mother covers that, or I cover that. Once in awhile Christy will cover that, but mainly my mother and I cover any properties that need to be shown to other agents that are by appointment.

When you go on a listing appointment do you always go, or does Christy go with you sometimes, as a husband and wife team?

Well, that's a great question; I'm glad you asked me that. One of our secrets is that I figure we get 75 percent of the listings we go out on. One of the things Christy has done she's made this magnificent presentation book which, I should have brought you a copy, I have one in my car. It's spectacular; I have never seen anything as good as this book. It divides up all of the areas that they have interest in, and people are usually really impressed. But, when I leave there if I have a sense that they're not going to list with us, or if they're not committing, then I will make an appointment for Christy to go, and she's so personable that she just sweet-talks them. Now she does not talk about business much; I mean she'll talk about pricing if she needs to but she generally talks about advertising and just gets to know the people and often that will win them over. Ninety percent of the time I go by myself and do the listing presentation by myself. The only time they meet Christy is when she goes out for the photoshoot or to do some advertising things.

My mother runs our office. She does most of the paperwork that needs to be done and keeps up with the files. Although I'm messing with the files; we're both messing with the files every single day. My brother takes overflow buyers. If I get sign calls or ad calls, and I don't have time, or I'm not interested in the call, I'll give them to him.

Q

And you take a referral off of that?

Yes, I take a 50 percent referral off of that. We pay my mother $12 an hour, and then we give her bonuses based on how we are doing. There is nothing set or concrete on the bonuses, it's just whenever there's some extra dollars around. We also have my aunt, my mother's sister, working for us. She does all of our mailings. She does addressing and all that kind of thing. And then Christy has that college girl who helps her out sometimes, then Steven is just on a referral basis and runs his own business.

Q

Kind of a buyer's rep on a referral basis?

On a referral basis only; exactly. My aunt works for us very part-time, maybe 10 hours a week, and this college girl works for Christy maybe 10 hours a week. That's about it. And, of course, all of us are licensed except my aunt and that college girl.

Q

So your mom does not go on listing appointments or show property or anything?

Well, she'll show property for me if I'm working with a client, and they're in town for three or four days, and they need to go out ever single day. On some days if I can't make it then she'll take them.

Q

Now let's talk a little bit about company support. How much office space do you and your team occupy? Either square feet or number of desks.

The single room that we occupy is probably 12 × 15 feet; probably about 200 square feet, and there's three desks placed in there.

Q

Do you feel that's adequate for your business now, or do you see growing out of it at some point?

I think that's wonderful space. I love that space. The only way that we would ever grow out of that is if my relationship with my brother changed; for example, if he got out of real estate, I might really hire somebody, a buyer's rep who works for us full time. In that case, I'm not exactly sure how we would facilitate that, but I don't see my brother getting out of real estate right now. Anyway, the space is just fabulous, and it's very nice ample space and, a good place.

Q *What benefits does the company provide to you and your staff, if any? Things like advertising, supplies, company paid staff help, accounting services for your team, special marketing incentives, or anything like that.*

I think Long Realty is the 'shiniest car' in town right now. Over the years it has been Tucson Realty and then Coldwell Banker, and now it's Long Realty that is the place to be. There's virtually nobody in town who has not at least heard of Long Realty. I mean they'd have to be blind to not see our signs and our advertising.

Q *A market share of over 40 percent does tend to get one's attention.*

I don't have to apologize for who the company is. If I'm competing against any other real estate company in town, there's an advantage just because I'm with Long Realty. Just being with the company is a fabulous advantage, and this company frees me up to be a selling machine, which is what I am. I can focus on being a selling machine and not have to worry about accounting much.

Q *Does the company take care of the accounting and payroll stuff for your team?*

Yes, they take care of it. She just sends them her time card, and they pay her out of my checks. I don't even know how many hours she's working; she just sends it over there and they take care of it. You know, it's nice having your mom work for you because you trust your mom. So Christy has also said that the advertising programs that Long Realty provide are wonderful too. I'm sure you'll hear this on Thursday when we get together for lunch; she's one of the greatest supporters of the Long programs. There are some times where we feel like we're supporting an issue of the company magazine because we've got so many ads in it, but we get the calls, you know, and they're a good deal because the company gets us price breaks off of them. So we use all that stuff.

Bob, you writing a book and talking to real estate agents about becoming a machine, a real estate machine, they better think about just selling real estate, and they better not think about doing any form of management. So, if they have their own company, if they open a little boutique, and they're doing management of any type; that will greatly take away from the effectiveness of their machine.

I couldn't agree more! The moment you get more than three people, your time is suddenly not your own to some degree, and it diminishes exponentially when you get more salespeople.

Frankly, Bob, that's how I got distracted last year. I'd been back in sales for 7 years. We got better every single year for 7 years. I mean, we did more business and then last year I started feeling a little guilty. I was on no Boards of Directors, I was not active in the community at all, and I made the mistake of getting on three Boards of Directors, and I just lost my focus, and I realized that last October or November. There weren't any sales happening. Of course, that was after September 11th, I mean I realized what was going on, and I quit everything. I resigned and went back to selling real estate.

Tell me about the company-paid support staff that the office has. How efficient do you think they are, and what role do they play in helping you do what you do, if they do at all?

Well, the office staff just augments my own personal staff. I hope that I don't put too much of a burden on them; I don't think I do; they don't ever complain to me too much. But, the nice thing about them is if I need something, if my mother is not here, I can call them, and they can get me what I need. Often the fact that they get a fax in and page me is so valuable because I can call in here and have them read something on the fax that I need, and I can say, "Can you turn around and fax that for me to this fax number?" It's amazing, Bob, that the nice thing about selling is that I can office wherever I am. I really can. If I'm in my car by myself with my phone, I have everything I need,

I have a whole office in my car. I have every form in my car; I have a computer in my car; I have an MLS computer in my car through the Palm Pilot. I use that Pocket Real Estate. I have my entire inventory and whatever I need, between me and my car, my mother and the front desk staff, I get done whatever I need to get done such that when I go home at night I have left hardly any work at the office. I mean I have the next day's work, but I don't have this sense that there's something I should have done or a phone call that I should have made. I go home. I try to get all that done so I can go home and relax.

Q

So the office staff really serves as an augment to what you would consider a self-contained business.

That's exactly right.

Q

Give a couple of opinions and view points if you will. Producing the very high sales volume that you produce every year clearly sets you apart from the average real estate agent. What do you do that is so effective and different from them?

I think we do several things that are different from what other people do. But, it would be so easy for every one of them to change to what we do that I consider a principal cause for us selling the volume that we do. Number one, I am very jealous of not being able to answer my phone and about the only time that I turn my phone off is if I'm doing a listing presentation. Even when I go back to take the listing, they're already mine; I already got them, so they can listen to me answer the phone. But... and I will apologize, I say, 'I answer my phone when I'm on some other appointments. Somebody calls off of your sign, and you want me answering the phone.' And I attribute a lot of our difference to the fact that I am so available. I get a lot of calls from real estate agents wanting information because they know that I'll give it to them. I have the MLS number of every one of my listings with me; I give them the MLS number; they look it up and maybe go and show my listings and sell them.

Q

You clearly generate more showings of your listings that way.

Absolutely. So the other thing is that I have my own signs. They have my cell phone number on it so that all sign calls come directly to me.

Q   *Is that the only number on the sign?*

That's the only sign; that's the only number. Except for the Web site, I have my own Web site. So on all of my ads it's my cell phone number; I don't have any calls come into the office here with the exception of the calls that are generated by the MLS listings, you know, where you have to have the office number on there. But any sign calls and ad calls go to my cell phone. It was because I answered the phone that I was able to sell my own listing last year for $1.8 million. If I hadn't taken that call, I may not have gotten the appointment.

Q   *How true, and you can't help but wonder just how many calls on your listings get blown by unprepared floor agents when you have a sign on the property with the company number on it.*

They called; I answered, made an appointment, and sold the house in two days. A $1.8 million dollar double-dip and I can point to situations like that a lot. I think that is a really, really important thing. The other thing is to position yourself; I was telling Mary about this. I said, 'Mary, it's no harder to sell a $150,000 house than it is to sell a $650,000 house. It just depends on where you place yourself. Are you going to place yourself where there are $150,000 buyers and $150,000 sellers, or are you going to place yourself where there are $650,000 buyers and sellers.' Because if you hold $650,000 open houses, then the people who are going to come are considering buying those, or they're considering selling their own that is approximately like that, and they want to see what the competition is. So, we have placed ourselves amongst those upper-end buyers that increase our volume exponentially.

Q   *So basically you have made a very concerted effort to decide where you wanted to go and then you just wrote out a business plan to get you there.*

Well, no, I wouldn't say that. I would say that it just started to happen. When we started to sell again in 1994 it was not our intent to work the upper-end market. It just started happening. And as it started to happen we began to recognize that it was happening and why it was happening and so now we do what we need to do to maintain it.

So the recognition of why it was happening probably is a key factor there.

Yes, that right.

It started out accidentally almost, and you were astute enough to say to yourself, 'this is happening; how do we progress with this?'

That's exactly right.

Is there anything else that you think makes you effective and different?

Well, I think the fact that we spoil our clients. Some of them do recognize it. You know they do, like that letter you got, that you read today. I've got stacks of those things, and I put them in our listings presentations. So, I think the fact that we spend a reasonable amount of money; we are always available; if one of my sellers calls me, nine times out of ten I answer the phone; and if I don't, I'm generally back to them within two hours so you know they tell their friends about us.

In your opinion, what is the single biggest benefit that you bring to your client?

Well, I wrote down two reasons. The single biggest benefit?

You could have more than one that's equally beneficial.

Well, I said exposure and experience. Getting optimum exposure of their property for them.

Q

So your marketing and advertising program, and the follow up and high degree of personal attention to the calls that come in off of your marketing efforts is the combination that brings in a lot of business?

Yes, and once we get it sold, or once we get it into a negotiation stage, the fact that we've been doing this for a while is a major factor in the overall success.

Q

Tell me where you see the residential real estate agent's role in the home buying process going in the next several years?

That's a really interesting question. I think the Internet has changed our role a little bit, and I tell that to sellers when I'm doing a listing presentation. It hasn't made it necessarily better or worse; it's made it a little bit different. It used to be that nine times out of ten, a buyer found their house because of the real estate agent, but now, not only is the real estate agent looking for the house, but more buyers are using the Internet to find houses. So, in my opinion there's probably a much greater likelihood today that the buyer is going to find their dream-home than there was fifteen years ago. I would guess that 15 years ago the buyers settled for fewer options than they do today. Today, they can be searching as much as the real estate agent, or more.

Q

They seem to come to the realtor at the point that they want the realtor involved to help them in negotiations and things. They seem to come to them better informed, and I see the transactions going a little bit smoother. Do you agree with that? With the Internet buyers because they seem to have eliminated a lot of the homes, they seem to have gathered enough information to where it's different than working with a buyer who hasn't done that.

Yes, but I still get a lot of buyers who are very comfortable searching the Internet while I'm searching the Multiple Listing Service; it's like we work as a team. You know if there here on a buying trip, and they're looking for four days, then they're bringing me things they want to see; I'm showing them things I think they should see. Between the two of us we really do a good job on the market. But, will that ever eliminate the need for a real estate agent? No. I can't imagine that, because they can't get in the homes. You know, sellers are not going to hire a machine to market their house for them. A machine can't open the door, a machine can't write the contract. So I don't see that changing in the near future.

I agree with that. It used to be that our value came from having a 'lock' on the inventory; that simply isn't enough anymore. I've heard it said several times that our value today comes so much more from our negotiating skills and marketing skills. Would you agree with that?

I certainly do; absolutely!

What are the top three pieces of advice that you can give to a real estate agent that wants to become a mega-producer?

All right, number one, answer your phone. I was just with John McCaleb of McCaleb Construction, and we were trying to get in touch with a real estate agent who had just sold one of my listings, and we needed some information about some repairs. I'd been trying to get her all day long. For half a day I have not been able to get this agent, and I said, 'You know, John, why don't these people answer their phones?' I said that to him because I know that he has a construction business, and he always answers his phone. He said, 'In my little company we have 12 cell phones, everybody answers their phone.' So, number one answer your phone.

Number two, work hard. The beauty of this business, I used to be a schoolteacher, and I got paid an additional $600 a year for being a speech coach all year long. Going to speech meets on the weekend and after school, $600. So as a teacher you did not get paid what you were worth. In real estate you get paid according to how you work; if you work extra time, you're going to get paid for it. If you work hard, if you just keep going back every day you'll be successful.

Number three, give people more than they expect. So they're surprised. I like to surprise people. They come into my open house, and they expect to be badgered by a real estate agent and to find out information about the house. They come into my open house, and I don't ask them for their name; I don't ask them to sign in; I give them a *Homebuyer's Guide* magazine with my card attached to it. On the inside is a package of listings, the house that I'm sitting, and then every other house that's for sale in the neighborhood. So they walk out; they haven't been badgered; they found out about the house; they know about the entire neighborhood. So give them more than what they anticipate, and the same thing with a sign call or an ad call. They call you on your sign, and they expect you to try to land them as a client, and they expect to get the information about the house. So, you do not try to land them as a client, but you offer to mail them a booklet of all of the properties for sale in the subdivision. They get more out of that phone call than they anticipated. So, surprise people by giving them more than they anticipated.

Is there anything else that you'd like to tell the person reading this book?

Well, yes. When I was a high school teacher I thought that I was educating myself, and I remember my first year in real estate so opened my eyes. Teachers live in a closet.

Really?

Absolutely! In that first year I would compare the careers, and I thought in teaching you learn some things from fellow teachers, you learn things from students and from personal relationships, but you get those same things from your clients and your peers. In teaching you learn from books; here you learn from experience, you learn from reading, you learn from continuing education, but you learn about law intimately, banking, finance, economics, even politics. You know, probably 75 percent of politics is what to do with the land. So real estate is really one of the last vestiges of the free enterprise system, and not only can you earn what you're worth, but there is never a day that goes by that you don't learn. People say to me, 'well, you probably know it all.' No way! Maybe I know 60 percent, and that 60 per cent is constantly changing. So, it's a fabulous occupation, you just have to work hard.

Interview with David Vanneste—Edina Realty, Minneapolis, Minnesota
2002 Sales volume in excess of $42 million.

Bob Herd's comments are in bold and italicized type.
David Vanneste's reponses are in regular type.

David, let's start with your background. What did you do prior to your real estate career?

I was a college student managing kind of a high-end restaurant in our local market area.

Really? That's interesting.

Yeah, Originally, I started there as a busboy and dishwasher in high school. I started waiting on tables, which was a perfect college student job because you know, you make good tips, and it helped to pay my tuition, and I could take spring break as my vacation.

Then I went into a management position to get business experience because I was in the Carlson School of Management at the University of Minnesota. I met a young guy there who was a young builder; a very successful young man. He would come in a lot of times at night around 9:30 p.m. or so for dinner, and we became friends. It was about the same time that I used to eat because things were winding down by then. So, he was the impetus that got me into the real estate business.

Was he a Realtor?

No, he was a builder, but he wanted me to work for his company, but that didn't fit the business plan that I had for my life. I was a marketing major and wanted a sales career so he said 'Why don't you come and sell houses for me?'

He wanted to open his own brokerage company because he was looking at all the money that he was paying to the real estate agents that were marketing his properties, so he had me start selling homes for him with the idea that after 2 years I would become the broker of his company.

What an interesting way to start in the business!

What ended up happening was that he didn't want to wait the two years, so he ended up moving forward with someone else, then I left the small 'mom-and-pop' operation and went to work at a bigger brokerage company where I felt more comfortable.

Did that work well for you?

Yes, it actually did. Probably the biggest decision that people in my first office were making every day when they arrived at around 11:00 a.m. was where they were going for lunch. Nobody had any kind of real business plan, so I felt that I would have more direction and focus at one of the bigger brokerages where I could see how it's really done, so that's how I started, right out of college in my early twenties.

So that's how you actually decided on a real estate career?

Yes, I actually got licensed on a Friday and sold my house on the immediate following Sunday. I did the math, and I thought 'wow! This is more than I make in salary in 2 months, so I was hooked at that point. It was kind of a kooky deal, but we were working a model home, and we had three models. After watching these other two salespeople for 2 days, someone pulled up in a rusty car, and they nudged each other and said, 'Well, let's give this one to David.' I knew what I was doing, I studied all of the material, but we walked down to one of the models and never came back. Those guys thought 'What the heck happened?' It turned out that those people bought the model, completely furnished, and it drove the other guys crazy. It was kind of fun!

So you knew people as well as you knew your product, even then?

Yeah, I guess I did.

Q *When did you start in real estate?*

In 1986, so I'm about a 17-year veteran.

Q *Which company are you with now?*

I am with Edina Realty in Minneapolis Saint Paul, Minnesota.

Q *David, tell me a little about your family. Your wife and kids, things like that.*

My wife was actually my business partner for many years. We ran as a team, one of the first husband and wife teams in our market area. She no longer is active in the business. She is licensed but hasn't done any real estate work at all for probably three years.

Q *My wife did the same thing when the kids got to be that certain age; I've never regretted it one bit.*

Sure. So, let's see, we got married about the same time I started in the real estate business, so we've been married about 16 years, and we've got a 14-year-old, a 12-year-old, a 14-month-old, and we are now expecting our fourth.

Q *Oh, no kidding, huh? You've got a big spread between them.*

Yeah, we went all the way back. We're actually enjoying the heck out of that.

Q *I have a granddaughter that I'm just thoroughly in love with. She'll be 14 in April of this year. My kids are all in their late-twenties to mid-thirties.*
OK, let's talk about your business for a little while. What, on average, has your sales volume been over the last three to four years?

We're holding in the mid-40 million dollar range. $40 million to $45 million, somewhere in that range.

About how many units does that represent a year?

We're running about 150 to 170.

You're the perfect person to round out this book because that's the sector that I have not covered yet; you know, the really high-volume number of units.
On average, and given the different market conditions encountered in recent times, is your volume going up or down each year?

What I have found with our sales volume is that we'll hit a certain plateau and then we will make a big jump ahead exponentially. If I go back, I can remember early on doing $3 million in sales and thinking, 'that was good,' and then all of a sudden the next year I jumped to $6 million and then to $12 million and then I remember going to $15 million and $20 million.

It seemed like the last move that we made was getting out that mid-20s, right up to the mid-40s and doing that in just a couple of years. It's one of those things where, if you do everything the same you're going to do about the same every year, but for me, it's just adding more staff people, getting better systems in place, better marketing. Making decisions about people faster and not wasting time with non-productive people has become extremely important. So we've been kind of at this plateau right where we are for about three years. Prior to that, we were probably doing about $30 million a year so we did a big jump there.

I'll say; a big monstrous 33 percent jump!

And, I think that if I get everything really clicking, our team could really be pushing $60 million without making a lot of major changes; maybe adding one more buyer representative.

OK, I'm going to talk about your staff in a little while but it certainly sounds like your annual business planning includes analyzing your staff, where you want to go and what kind and size staff that you need to get there. Then you seem to refine your activities and the activities of your staff; is that an accurate statement?

Yes, some of that, and I think also analyzing the staff and looking at the market, you know, what we've strategically done once we've gotten into an area where we are one of the dominant players, and we're trying to look around and say, 'OK, what makes sense to us?' What market should we expand into now? Often, it's going into another suburban area. We're in kind of the middle of the third-tier rings of the suburbs in the city. You've got the inner-city first tier, which would be like homes typically built in the 1930s, 1940s, and the 1950s, and then you get the second-home market areas, then the third home areas. That's where we are really dominant.

So you're just expanding outward from the core part of the inner city?

That's right, expanding outward you know trying to keep our core area, but then expanding. Looking at the market—what makes sense to expand into—and we've given up some markets where maybe the sales prices are not as high. We're not putting as much emphasis there and maybe going into some different markets that are more profitable.

Not enough overall results for the efforts?

That's right.

When you started in real estate, then became what I'm calling a mega-producer that hits or exceeds the $30 million mark, how many hours a week did you work in an average week? Let's say when you started versus when you attained the $30 million mark?

I probably worked less when I started just because I didn't have the business out there, although I did almost everything myself. What's kind of ironic is that I actually work less hours today than I ever have, and I make a lot more money, which is kind of a nice thing. I would say on average right now I'm working maybe 50 hours a week. Probably when I was working the most was when I was doing about $6 million to $10 million but I didn't have the support staff then.

> **Q**
>
> *That seems to follow a definite trend that I'm seeing in all of you.*

I was probably putting in 60 to 70 hours a week when the market was really hot; just nonstop, you know?

> **Q**
>
> *I sure do! That's a very strong trend that I have seen in all four of the interviews. That's really interesting; great information.*
>
> *When you began your real estate career, did you have a business plan? If you did, how has it evolved over the years?*

When I first started I did not have a real plan just because I was primarily doing site sales. I quickly got bored with that because, you know, it's just too passive, and a lot of times no one shows up, so your day is wasted.

> **Q**
>
> *Yes, it's like a perpetual open house.*

Once I moved over to Edina Realty, I quickly looked at the business and analyzed who the players in our market were at that time. You know, the big mega-agents who were doing maybe 10 million dollars to 12 million dollars. There were very few primary breadwinners in our market. So I was probably one of the first agents in our company to really look at who the players were and analyze what they were doing. We're a very large company and we were slow to get computerized.

My business plan started with doing some marketing with funds that I didn't have, a lot of times on credit cards, did some door-to-door prospecting and kind of started small in farming. We got computerized so that we could do more farming, and we started with a neighborhood of about 300 homes, and now we're farming 10,000 homes.

> **Q**
>
> *Do you have an outside company that does the mailings for you?*

Yes, we don't do that ourselves any more. That was part of those hours in the early days of licking envelopes, and we would actually cut and paste on the copy machine and run them off. You know, whatever we could do low-budget. Then we started using a printer and developed an image. Today, my key assistant and I probably work on the next year's budget off and on for about two weeks every December. We set up the entire next year and know exactly how much we are spending.

So you have your detailed budget in place prior to the beginning of each new year, and you know where all of the money is going.

Exactly.

And is part of those two weeks spent analyzing where last year's money was spent, how effective it was, and where you can adjust for maximum return?

It sure is, and our business plan will evolve as the year goes by. There are times where we may even stop sending some stuff out because I can't handle all the appointments I have coming in. So I might just say, back off a notch. And there are other times when we step it up because we're not as busy as we want to be, so we adjust the timing of some of the things that we do. We use technology a lot. I can't remember a time in the last 10 years when I haven't had computers or something on the tax return. You know, we keep up with technology. We've embraced it, and we use it to our advantage. We've done a pretty good job of maintaining our past clients database and that has been a significant factor in our success. Farming is a big part of our business plan; we do a lot of direct mail. We probably spent more on direct mail than most agents make in a year.

That's another trend that I'm seeing, and I want to explore the subject of how much of your gross income you spend on marketing and advertising. I'm hearing things from other mega-producers about that subject that are very, very similar. Can you tell me about how much of your gross income you spend on marketing and advertising?

It's right around 15 percent.

Q

> *That's really interesting. I'm hearing 14 percent to as high as 18 or 19 percent, so you're right in the middle.*

And actually, if I looked at the last 2 years, I'd say that 15 percent will be a pretty strong average for the last 5 years. Over the last couple of years that's actually gotten closer to 10 percent because as the business has grown our expenses have stayed fairly fixed. So it's kind of nice, that last $200,000 can be kind of a bonus.

Q

> *Do you work a specialty market or niche market?*

Well, we specialize more in a geographic area. We do have several areas that we specialize in; one would be Lakeshore. We're in the area, Minnesota 10,000 lakes. We're in a suburban area where within a six- or eight-mile radius we have five or six premier full recreational lakes.

Q

> *Wow!*

A lot of Lakeshore. I currently live on a lake, and that helps I think. So I would say in a couple of lakes very few transactions have happened without us being involved.

Q

> *Do you have a special group that you market to that are all lakeshore residents?*

Yes, we do a little bit. One part of our farms are broken down geographically, but we do have one that's specifically just lakeshore. Then we've got a high-end market. I belong to a country club in the area called North Oaks. It's a private community with acreage type lots and high-end homes. I do a lot stuff in that market, and then as a team we're probably the biggest player in our immediate suburb by about a five-to-one margin over our nearest competitor.

Q

> *How did you evolve into working those types of specialty areas? Did you just start working them and time-block some of your time and*

do activities that got you known in those areas slowly, over time, or just how did you do it?

Actually, that is how we did it. We started with about a 300-home neighborhood where we were living at the time in the early 1980s and then we just analyzed the MLS data each year. We would say, 'Jeez, look at how many homes are turning over in this area,' and we would go to work there. We also track average market time as I think that it is a key indicator of coming activity in an area. Once we became dominant in a neighborhood and had at a strong market share, we would try to pick up similar types of neighborhoods. One of the best things that we've used is the 'Just Listed' postcard and 'Just Sold' postcard program. You can take like-kind homes and switch to a similar type of neighborhood and the homes are nearly the same so people don't know the difference. I guess what I am saying is we try to work around the sold signs and try to increase our business off of them.

That's an interesting way to magnify your business. After you became dominant in a neighborhood, then moved into a new neighborhood, what would you do to maintain your dominance in the existing neighborhood?

Well, we would never stop with the mailings. That's probably a big part of it. So we would continue to maintain our presence via direct mail and signage. Our signage is also a big part of our success and market dominance. I have a name rider that is about half the size of the sign that's on the house. The company doesn't like it, but that's too bad. We were also one of the first agents to have a photo rider. One of the questions that I always ask people is what made you call us or why did you call us? The biggest response I've gotten from people is 'well we always see your sign and it always says sold.' So since I always kept hearing that, I thought, 'I've got to differentiate our signs even more to make it stick out.' So, we've done that to make the sign stick out even more, and it's really helped.

When you say 'we' on the signs and advertising items, is it your picture, or yours and your wife's picture?

It's my wife and I.

> *That's great information, you see, Russell Long and his wife, Christy, who are here in Tucson do the same thing. Russell is the number one agent in Southern Arizona and does about what you have been doing, around $40 million or so a year. His wife doesn't actually sell any longer, but she generates a huge amount of their business through social circles. They still use both of their pictures on everything that they do; it's very interesting to see the similarity between you two.*

Well what I figure is we built such a strong brand name over time and earlier in our career we used to both go on listing appointments, you know, every single one. You start looking at each other and you say 'We're wasting time, we don't both need to be here.' But once you've built that brand name you just don't change it. People sometimes say to me, 'You know, your wife isn't working that much with you any more, and she's still on your staff.' I say, 'Of course, look at the mistake that Coca-Cola made when they went to Coke Classic. Once you're a brand name you don't change it.'

> *Exactly. Now I have a couple of other questions about that. What percentage of your business is listings versus sales?*

We're about 60/40. Sixty percent on the listing side.

> *About what percentage of your business comes from these following areas?*
> *Referrals.*

About 25 percent.

> *How much is from marketing? In other words, magazines and other image-building type of media versus advertising.*

This is a tough one to really break down, but we're figuring about 40 percent on the marketing and then about 35 percent on the mailing.

OK; then how much on advertising? That would be Web sites, newspapers, home for sale type magazines, realtor.com, and things like that.

I kind of put that in with the marketing.

A lot of people do, but they are really very different in the results that they achieve. You will always get some sales from marketing, but marketing vehicles such as upscale magazines, billboards, brochures that tell about you and your team, and other things like that are clearly different from *Homes & Land* magazine or the area newspaper real estate section in what they actually achieve.

Now that you mention it, you're right, they really are different.

Do you do telemarketing or cold-calling?

No.

You don't have anyone on your team that does?

No I don't.

That's fine. Some do; some don't. I have actually found that the majority of people that are working at your level of production don't either. You said that you use mailings to both stabilize and build your business instead, right?

That is correct.

OK, well, you described your marketing and advertising program for me in our previous discussion so I'm going to skip over that. Anything else about your marketing and advertising that you would like to ad?

Well, a couple of things that we did early on; we bought a big chunk of the cover of the local phonebook, which was a good image piece for us. We're on about a half dozen benches in our market area. We've had those a long time; they have the same logo as our signs so it's kind of combining a lot of that stuff. We'll probably come back to some of the specialty things, but we do an annual full report that is a real nice marketing piece.

Q   *Now that is really interesting because Hugh Cornish does the same thing and says that it is very effective.*

Q   *Do you sponsor any events or anything?*

No, we don't do that, but the other big thing that we do is, my kids go to a private Catholic school, and their fundraiser every year is called the marathon. The day before the marathon, we deliver water bottles to all the kids and students at the school. That's been a huge image-building piece for us. We also order a bunch of those for the local kid carnivals for the different elementary schools in our area.

Q   *We talked initially that about 15 percent of your gross income was allocated to marketing, advertising, and image-building and that you've got it heading toward the 10 percent mark. Is that right?*

Yes, that's correct.

Q   *How do you track that? How do you track its effectiveness?*

Well, there's a couple things that we do. We track all of the buyer calls that come in.

Q   *For source?*

Yes, for source. We try to track those for source and who takes the call and conversion rate. So I can run a conversion rate on my buyer agents. That's one way you get a pretty good gauge, and then we send out a prelisting packet that's very comprehensive, and I'll send you a copy of that. We also send a questionnaire out. So if you call my office today and say, 'David we're thinking about selling our house,' by the time you get home from work that will be sitting on your doorstep.

Oh, OK, and there's something in the package that asks what made them call you?

Yes. We ask them a bunch of questions about why there's selling. I try to probe for price and motivation. There are a couple of times in there that asks them pretty directly why did you call us? You know, what made you call me today? That really helps me to get a gauge of what works in the marketplace.

You take a 2-week period during the holiday season to plan for the next year. Is this a time when you and your team or specific members of your team carefully go over this data and then decide where you are going to allocate your advertising and marketing dollars the following year?

That's right, except that we also monitor it quarterly as well.

Can you supply me with some copies of your marketing and advertising pieces?

Yes.

What I would like to do with them is to shrink them down to fit this book and then use them as examples for the readers so just anything that you think would be appropriate would be nice. I would like to have things that people would look at and say, 'Gee, that's a nice piece, I'd like to do something like that.'

What programs or methods do you have in place to retain past clients and receive referrals from them?

Well, all of our past clients are maintained on a database. We do contact them regularly. We have a part of our marketing program that we call our 'sphere list' versus our farm areas. Some of these people are on both lists so they're going to get an inundation of mail from us. We try to send our past clients helpful stuff several times of the year so direct mail is our primary source of staying in touch. Over the last 10 or 15 years, I have developed most of the really close friends that I have as clients first and the friendships grew from there; it's fun!

Q

You know, I'm the same way, and all of the high-producers that I've talked to say the same thing! That seems to run through all of the really good agents; it's amazing, isn't it?

You know, it's one of those things. We're very social people, and I think you've got to stay in touch with many of those people. You've got your core group that you have dinner with a few times a year or do different things and they're going to be one of your big referral sources.

Q

Do you ever follow any of the programs out there by people like Mike Ferry or Brian Buffini or any of those guys?

I've not studied a lot of Mike Ferry stuff. I have been invited; I actually had thought about going down to one of those things this past month. He invited me to come down as one of the top agents and just take his course for free.

Q

I have been through Brian Buffini's course three times. The first time that I went through his course I had 28 referrals in 10 months. Most of them came in the last four to five months, though.

I've done more training with Howard Brinton. Most of my team members have done one of his university programs. He's got a good team-training program. It really sets up your team to understand the role of the rainmaker and what their role is in trying to work together.

Q

Oh, really! He's ahead of the rest of the sales trainers then because that's something that's very necessary today, and there simply isn't enough of that type of training out there.

Yeah, and I think it's good too, because he also has a buyer specialization course that I've sent my buyer agents to, and I think what really is helpful for them is that it gets them thinking bigger. I think that's important. One my guys that went through one of his courses and could see that there are guys out there that make four or five times my income and he got a real 'I can do this attitude.' He's also got good scripting and good planning stuff. I thought his course was really good.

How many people do you have in your database?

Our sphere of past clients is about 1,800. I know that sphere of past clients number because we're doing a Christmas CD that we're sending out to all of them through a company. It was actually very reasonable. I think that for 1,800 pieces it was under $4 in the mail with a nice card. The CDs got our name and stuff on it.

Does the relationship that you have with people affect the way that you contact them?

Yes.

So is it more personal with the sphere of influence people than it is with your general farming type of mailings?

That is right.

You just talked about the Christmas things. One of my questions is: Do you send items of value, such as the CD, to your client database on a regular basis to provide a service and maintain contact?

Yes, that's something that we're just trying this year. We also send out a magnetic calendar each year. Those go to all of our past clients and all of the current home areas that we are farming. The other thing that people really like is the little notepads that we send out. They are about 3-inches by 8 ½ inches and have about 30 sheets. They are very inexpensive, and I get them from a guy in Denver. You can slip them right into a regular size-10 envelope.

Exactly, I did that same thing very early in my career, and I also found it to be very effective.

Those kind of things such as notepads and magnets have a good shelf-life. They stay around. They're sitting by the phone in the kitchen or on the refrigerator.

Q

I couldn't agree more. Do you do anything with the college football schedule?

No, we don't do anything like that. We have incorporated the Viking's schedule, like this year, we actually did the Vikings and the Packers in the same mailing as one of our post cards. So we'll maybe do that. Most of our mailing stuff is postcards by the way, just because you don't have the envelope.

Q

Do you have your team doing these mailings, or do you have someone else doing them for you?

The team does them for me on a regular basis. We've got a marketing company that prints everything and sends it out; we just kind of direct it. Heidi from my office, who is my primary assistant, directs all of our marketing and manages all of our listings, so she and I will be the ones who sit down and go through budget and set up our marketing plan for the year.

Q

How long has she been with you?

She's been with me for 4 years.

Q

Let's talk about your team. You've obviously built a highly effective team. How many people do you have on your team?

I've got two licensed assistants and two buyer's agents.

Q

So there is a team of five, and if you include your wife, then there's six of you.

Right, exactly.

Two of you as rainmakers and four support people. Tell me a little about the buyer's reps' role.

We work on a commission split, and basically anything that comes through, you know a buyer calls, I pass on to them. We use a software system that is an automated e-mail-based buyer tracking system. Right now, between my two buyer's agents, we've got 130 buyers on that program. It's a pretty easy sell. Basically, a call comes in off of a sign, newspaper, magazine, or whatever, and we forward that call directly to Heidi, my assistant, and then to one of the buyer agents. So basically all buyer calls that come in are fielded by one of those two people, unless I just happen to answer the phone. So they work primarily with most of my buyers; I work with very few buyers. I work almost exclusively on the listing side.

That is another very strong trend that I am seeing in all of you mega-producers.

I'll typically work with some people that were good past clients or maybe a very high-end buyer, but only if I've got a good strong personal relationship with them.

Then you have Heidi and another person. They are both licensed, so everyone on your team is licensed, right?

Yes, I've got two buyer-agents, and they did five to seven million apiece last year in sales. Then Heidi runs all of my marketing stuff; she's on a salary plus a bonus so she gets salary plus benefits from me. I pay a car allowance, a cell phone allowance. She also gets something on each sale that closes and that gets paid through the broker.

Edina does all of the bookkeeping for you for your team?

She just gets paid $100 per closing and that just comes off my commission.

Over and above her salary?

Over and above, right. That gets paid directly to her even if one of my buyer-agents sells something. My other assistant, Barb, is more of a closing manager and escrow trouble shooter. She also does signs and stuff like that. So her primary job is closing the escrow, you know, getting the loan, inspections, appraisals, final walk-through and making sure that keys are given and the signs and keyboxes are taken off.

So she really does almost the entire escrow and all of the 'client-friendly' stuff.

That's right.

So, no other team members, that's it?

Right, the buyer agents are independent contractors paid through the broker, and the other two are paid directly by me.

Are they paid on a referral fee basis from you, or is it a regular commission split where they get part of the sales volume and so do you?

That's exactly how it is. It's a normal split, and they run their own numbers and volume. We work on what Edina Realty calls a 90/10 plan where basically we're paying desk rent and retaining the majority of our commission dollars.

Long Realty has a 100 percent plan that accomplishes the same thing, but in a little different way.

Let's talk a minute about company support. How much office space do you and your team occupy?

Well, we have around seven to eight hundred square feet in three private offices. Heidi and I are in one, Barb and one of my buyer-agents are in another, and the third one is occupied by the other buyer-agents. The office building that we are in has three floors, and we are hoping to get more space on the third floor when the existing tenants move out. We would like to have about 1,500 square feet with kind of our own reception area and conference room. It might even be bigger than that.

That would give you additional square footage to add staff if you want to.

Yeah, add staff and take care of our biggest problem right now, which is storage. You know, you get 10 to 20 thousand pieces of printing stuff at a time for brochures and things like that, and there's just no place to put it. You don't want to bring it home because it's not accessible, then you run into humidity problems if paper isn't stored correctly.

The company provides benefits to you in handling your payroll issues and that type of thing. Do they provide any other type of benefits like additional advertising, supplies, or company-paid staff or help?

No, the biggest thing that they provide is the receptionist that sets up all of the showings; then you've got your sales and listing secretaries that process your listings and sales through the company and take care of the advertising. We hire out the payroll through a company called Paycheck.

So Edina Realty doesn't do your payroll for your staff then?

No, we handle that ourselves.

So that's probably the biggest thing is the support staff. People often ask me 'why don't you go out on your own and do your own deal?' Part of it is that I don't want to micromanage part-time jobs; you know, things like receptionists that don't show up on Sunday mornings and things like that.

That's what I do for a living. I know just exactly what you mean! I've actually been blessed with an amazing staff; really world-class.

Yeah, you know, it just isn't worth it for what the dollar advantage would be.

> *I had my own company in California for about 15 years and that's one of the reasons that I finally sold it and started managing for the larger companies; you had the support staff issues and all of the other stuff to deal with, and I got tired of doing it all by myself. I couldn't agree with you more.*

Yeah, I have a big enough headache just trying to deal with a couple of people.

> *I've got 177 agents and a support staff of seven; it keeps you very busy. There's no way that I could sell even if I wanted to. Those days are gone, but I do love what I do. I have a really special group of people in my office. We're very close.*

You know, we've got the office space in a nice building and all of the backup support. We have all of our own equipment. I wouldn't even know how to turn on one of the office computers. The copy machine is the only company things that we use.

> *Edina Realty has a wonderful reputation, so it sounds to me like a class-act company within a class-act company. That's a great combination. It sounds to me like that's what you have accomplished.*

That's exactly what we've done.

> *I would like to get your opinions and viewpoints on a couple of things. Producing the very high sales volume that you produce every year clearly sets you apart from the average real estate agent. What do you do that's so effective and different from the average agent?*

Obviously the longevity of the image building is a major part of that. I think that if you start from the time that you contact my office, through the closing, it's about systems; about how things and people are handled. It starts with the client getting a very professional prelisting packet delivered to their door the day they call me. It's about having an excellent marketing presentation and coming through strong at the listing appointment. In many cases, I go out to the house, and I don't have to say a thing; we just get right to it and sign the listing.

Other times I need to really sell myself and my high degree of service. I always tell the sellers that one of the most critically important things that they can do for themselves is to hire an agent with a large sphere of influence. That will have a major impact on how quickly their home will sell, and for how much money.

We really focus on dominance in that sphere of the market. At my listing appointments I kind of go into how we 'ping pong' people off of different houses for maximum effectiveness for them and for the sellers. Having a consistent advertising presence in the magazines and other media is very important. I stress that my team has more buyer calls than any other team in town, and they will benefit from that. Our follow up system is beyond excellent and that is a major advantage to our clients, and we let them know it on a consistent basis.

It sounds like you have a real hands-on, very close relationship from beginning to end with your clients with a lot of effective communication.

Good communication is a big part of our success. It can be tough in a slow market when the houses aren't selling, but it's still essential. You've got to take a lot more time, and you've got to have those face-to-face meetings with people when things are tough, and you've got to get price adjustments or whatever it takes to get their home sold.

We send out a survey to each client about a week to ten days into the listing. This gives us a gauge of what their expectations are and whether or not we are meeting them; again, it's a client satisfaction thing. It's a questionnaire that asks things like: Do they like the brochure that we have created? Are we communicating enough? Are they happy with the advertising? Then we follow up with feedback reports every ten days on every listing. Our buyers, and the co-op buyer's agents, are also sent questionnaires, and we use that feedback to help get price adjustments and suggest other necessary changes, like 'clean the carpets' or things of that nature. Once we have the listing, our clients are going to get something in the mail from us every week and that standard has really helped us to grow and maintain our business and reputation.

That's an excellent concept! In your opinion, what is the single biggest benefit that you bring to your clients?

That's a tough one, because sometimes it's a combination of everything that you do. I think that integrity plays a major role in it. You know, where you're really looking out for what's in the client's best interest. One of the nice things about getting to a certain level of business success in real estate is that whether you make a sale or not, it really doesn't matter, your next house payment isn't hanging on it, so you always have the client's best interest at the forefront.

Q

So maybe you can say that your marketing package as a whole, combined with a high degree of integrity produces a low-stress transaction for both your buyer and seller clients with great results?

Well said, that's true.

Q

Tell me where you see the residential real estate agent's role in the home buying process going in the next several years.

Well, I think that our market is going to continue to change a lot as it has been. You know, a few years ago a lot of people were saying that the Internet was going to replace the real estate agent, but it really hasn't. What it's done is it's made us a lot more efficient. I think that the Internet today makes the consumer and us, as agents, more efficient, saves us time, and makes us a lot more money. We aren't the gatekeeper of information any longer; now we are the counselors, so to speak, or interpreter of the information. Buyers today don't seem to wonder if there's something out there that we're not showing them or telling them about because they have access to all of it anyway. Now they're looking to us for our professional opinion about the information to help them make a good decision. I'm very comfortable with this new role.

Q

So you see our role shifting from sales agent to counselor.

Well, yes; an advisory type of role. You know, 'Am I making the right decision?' 'Is the value there?' Those kinds of questions are common now and are critical to our new role. I think that you are going to see a lot more pressure on commissions; we're seeing that now. There are also a growing number of companies out there that are trying to beat us to the customer then sell them back to us. The fees charged by many of the relocation companies are just way out of control.

Well, let's give something to the reader. What are the top three pieces of advice that you can give to a real estate agent that wants to become a mega-producer?

Well, let's see. You need to hire people in order to grow, and they have to be as dedicated as you are. Every time that I have added someone, my income has gone up by about four to five times what they cost me, so I think that's the big first step is to hire good people to do the nonselling tasks.

Consistency; I've found that it takes two to three years to develop a new market, and way too many agents give up before they have given it sufficient time, and they don't commit sufficient resources to it. It's about building an image and a reputation; essentially a brand name, and you just can't do something like that with one or two mailings. You need to think long-term or about two years, and you should plan to send at least 18 mailings in that 2-year period.

Then the third thing is to not lose perspective on life.

Do you mean maintain a balance in your life?

Yes, be balanced. Take time off. Spend time with your wife and kids and your family; otherwise you're going to burn out. I also think that you absolutely must reinvest in your business, so I guess that I've got four things.

That fine. Is there anything else that you would like to share with the person reading this book?

No, not really.

In my opinion you've given some great advice to our readers; especially the part about staying balanced while you build your career. Thank you.

It's been my pleasure. I take about five to six vacations a year. If you don't get out of town, you don't get away from it.

Interview with Hugh Cornish—Coldwell Banker, Menlo Park, California
2002 sales volume was in excess of $105 million.

Bob Herd's comments are in bold and italicized type.
Hugh Cornish's responses are in regular type.

Q

    Hugh, tell me a little about your background. What did you do prior to your real estate career?

Really, from day one my business career started in real estate, so I have done different types of real estate. I started off out of college working for a real estate syndicator and did property management, asset management, and acquisitions in the Midwest. I worked in Kansas City and Dallas. That was a very interesting experience. It was just pre-1986 right before the real estate tax laws changed.

Q

    I was just going to ask you that.

That was a real good introduction to understanding investment real estate and understanding the apartment business and shopping centers. Then after that I came back to California. I tried my hand at residential for two years. I felt inclined, because of my family background, to give it a shot. I think frankly that I wasn't mature enough to really take it seriously enough and to want to be successful at it.

Q

    How old were you at the time?

I was 25 years old. On the weekends when my friends were all having fun I was holding open houses, and I thought, gosh, I don't know if this is the kind of career choice I wanted to make. So I went out and did some interviewing to see if I wanted to stay in the real estate business and I ended up interviewing with Coldwell Banker Commercial. I took a job with Coldwell Banker Commercial in the training program. For me that was like going to boot camp; it was the best thing I ever did. I really look at that as the foundation of my real estate career. I worked under a very successful commercial broker who really taught me the ropes of the business. I spent about 15 months in an internship and did just about everything across the board, especially investments and leasing. I was called a runner; a classic 'runnership' where you do all the dirty work, and you didn't get a lot of glory for it, but it was really a wonderful learning experience. It was also a good beginning to work under somebody and have a mentor.

That would be a great learning experience.

Then I left commercial real estate, actually just when I started to kind of be successful. I got an offer from a developer to take a job in the commercial development and property management field, and I did that for about a year and realized that was not what I wanted to do. I actually decided at that point in my career to go back to residential. Spending time in commercial, I think that I realized that it was much less personal than I had expected. I really have always had a strong affection for houses, and it was hard to get warm and fuzzy about commercial buildings, so I made the switch. I think at that point in my life that was the right time to do it and that's where I've been ever since.

Wasn't it about 1991 when you started here in the Menlo Park office, because that's just a year or so before I resigned as the branch manager here?

Yeah, that's correct, and that was a good time to get into the business because the business was challenging to say the least. You know we had just come off the peak of '89, and the market was definitely in a... had hit bottom, and I think if there's any time to go into business it's when business is at it's worst. I think that's where you really learn.

That's for sure; you train under those circumstances; then you can do the good stuff while falling out of bed. Tell me a little bit about your family.

I'm married; I've got three children; and I've been married for 13 years. There's no doubt about it—my wife and my children are a great motivation in my life. Not so much to be financially successful, although that's part of it, but just to have a good balance and to want to work with people and really create a good legacy for what I do. I want to keep a good reputation in the community so that if my children want to go into the business, they will have that to build on. Those are some of my goals, at least personally, about my career.

Q   *O.K., lets talk about your business. What has your sales volume been the last three or four years?*

Over the last four years I have averaged over $100 million in sales a year. 2000 was the peak, and that was probably about $125 million, and I finished 2002 at over $100 million again.

Q   *How many units does that represent a year, approximately?*

It's varied between 28 and probably 35 units a year.

Q   *So definitely a high average sales price market.*

Yes, because of the average sales price in this area I've been able to have a greater volume with less units than probably most any other area in the country. It's much like many areas on the east coast.

Q   *On average, and given the changing market conditions, about how much is your sales volume going up each year, or is it fairly stable?*

It's fairly stable; it definitely peaked in 2000. The challenging thing is to kind of keep it stable because with real estate prices declining, your sales volume and commission volumes are bound to go down just based on sheer value of properties. So actually I've had to work a little harder the last two years to keep the volume up. It seemed to carry itself for a long time actually, and with the decline of real estate values I've had to work very hard to keep it up. That's been my goal every year, to exceed $100 million in sales volume.

Q   *That's a very impressive goal. When you started in residential real estate, how many hours a week did you work and then on average, and roughly how many hours a week do you work now?*

It really hasn't changed that much; I wish I could say that it has. It varies seasonally, but I would say that the first couple of quarters of the year that I probably am working 60 hours a week. You work a lot of nights, something that not everybody chooses to do, but I tend to get a lot done in the evening, and I always have evening meetings with clients. I find that I would rather do that than work on the weekends, personally. But as the fall comes up it usually drops somewhere between 45 to 50 hours a week, but rarely less than that.

When you began your real estate career, did you have a business plan, and if you did, how has it evolved over the years?

I did write a business plan. As I mentioned previously, I was fortunate to have a very good mentor in commercial real estate and that was one of the things he thought was very important to implement in every business strategy is to have an actual goal. Sit down and write your goals and how to accomplish them. Anyone can write down 'I'd like to sell 10 houses this month,' but the question is how do you accomplish it?

I have had a business plan every year. I try to review it once a quarter with my assistant. We're constantly trying to strive to not only reach those goals but also hopefully to create some new goals at the same time.

The luxury home market is obviously a niche market. Beyond that broad statement, do you work a specialty or niche market?

I would say yes. As you know, Bob, from being here as the branch manager, the property values are, on the average, much higher than anywhere else in the country. The reality for me, in order to get the type of sales volume that I have with the number of houses that I sell, I need to really focus on the high end market. I think it's been a longer period to get there than if I started in a lower-end market, but I knew that once I established myself that it would be no more work than any other price range. I have really focused on Atherton, which is the area that I've been the number one producing agent in, and that is an area that has, as you know, very high end homes. There are about 2,500 homes in Atherton, and the average sales price is very high. It's really varied because the market's changed so much recently. I was very focused in the beginning. I decided to be a large frog in a small pond and not spread myself too thin. I think that what happens to a lot of agents is that when they start, they get desperate, and they'll go anywhere; they're very reactive; they're wherever their client is pointing. I decided early on to really draw some boundaries, physically, meaning I work really five areas: Atherton, Woodside, Menlo Park, Palo Alto, and Portola Valley. But also mentally to draw some boundaries with clients saying to myself that if they wanted to me to go down to Los Altos Hills and spend a week with them, I wouldn't do it. I think it turned some people off not to go to Hillsborough; not to go to Burlingame; but I decided that I would be much better off and serve my clients better if I was an expert in the five areas that I specialized in.

So, essentially you really gained market dominance through specialization and some discipline.

Absolutely! I think it's extremely important. It benefits your client because it gives you great depth your market; it gives you good credibility in your market when you do a lot of business in the same area. People recognize your name; they recognize your success, and I think it builds confidence in your client relations. It's really a benefit to the client, and I think it makes the business, frankly, much easier.

From the time that you got the mindset to focus on 'narrow and deep' until you became the dominant force in your local market, how long did it take you to achieve that status?

It took awhile. Although I hoped it would happen overnight, it didn't. Sales can be very humbling. You know, you can set goals, and you can have great aspirations, but it takes time to gain credibility. I just kept my nose to the grindstone; I never looked up. I decided that I wasn't going give up. My goal was to be the number one agent in the office, and then the number one agent in a certain market, then hopefully and potentially one of the number one agents in the county. So I guess one could say that it's taken 11 years, because this past year was the first time I was the number one agent in San Mateo County overall in sales volume. It took a lot of years to do that, but it took about five years for me to really get established and to get my name out there where I was starting to get some repeat business.

Approximately what percentage of your business is listing versus sales?

I would say that it's probably 60 percent listings 40 percent sales. I've always enjoyed the listing aspect of the business more than the sales side, but let me back up. I've enjoyed them both; I've just found that the listing side of the business is more proactive. I can control the process much better, and I also enjoy the marketing aspect of the business. I think it's one of the really exciting parts of the business. I think if one is creative, one can really express one's creativity, and it's just something that I enjoy doing more than working with buyers.

That's very good advice. Lets talk a for a minute about marketing and advertising. Tell me a little bit about what percentage of your business comes from the different sources. How much of your business comes from referrals?

I would say that referral is probably 50 percent of my business at this point, but I've never backed off the marketing aspect. As a matter-of-fact I've increased it every year. This is the first year I've probably started to back off a little bit. I really feel it's important to saturate your market. I think that you should never rest on your laurels. It's very easy to cut back on marketing and promotions, but I think it's important to keep up with your competitors. I also think that when people stop seeing your advertising, they kind of forget about you. In any market there is always a number of competitive real estate agents, and you really have to be continually out there in the public eye.

Do you do a lot of the image-building type of advertising in the magazines, like the upscale magazines and things like that?

I certainly do. I made a decision a long time ago to advertise narrow and deep, much like my market share. I'm not trying to advertise in the *San Francisco Chronicle* because San Francisco is not my market, nor is the *San Jose Mercury*. I tend to advertise in the local papers. I tend to farm only the area that I happen to work with the exception of the investment community. I farm the investment community very strongly, especially venture capitalists and investment bankers. As you know in this area, we have a very large number of venture capitalists; maybe the largest number of them in the world. They're only a mile away and that's actually been a great resource for my business. I saturate that community by mail on a consistent basis, and they've been a great source of referrals.

So, part of your business plan was to identify that group as a source of business and then use media that focused on them very heavily?

Absolutely. I just really felt that a very direct approach with them was the most effective way to get to know them; it turned out to be true and has been a major part of my business.

Rather than broad-based newspaper ads that go all over the place?

Yeah, I think a more focused approach is important. I look at my marketing plan as kind of a pie. I think that you need to have the whole pie to be balanced, and you can't have a piece missing here and there and expect to really cover everything. I set out from the beginning to farm my markets through mail, and I'm going to advertise in the local paper. I'm also going to do some real distinct and direct marketing to very focused groups of people that both buy and sell what I have to offer, which is luxury homes.

Target marketing?

Target marketing, yes; and frankly, I find it much more efficient. I also find that groups of people such as investment counselors and estate attorneys are also groups that are an excellent source of business.

Do you have a Web site?

Yes, I have a Web site. I've had a Web site now for going on about six years. I was one of the first real estate agents that I'm aware of that had a Web site. I was skeptical when I first set it up, but that's because at the time most people, including me, were not using the Web that much. Of course, today it's very commonplace. One has to have one. I think that agents are really making a mistake by not having one. If you use the search engines and go to the areas I work, mine comes up, but more importantly, I wasn't doing it so much to attract new buyers as I was to be interactive with my existing clients. First of all, when I'm doing a listing they want to know that they are getting that type of exposure. My Web site is on all of my advertising, including all flyers, newspaper ads, and everything. I think that people enjoy going there to be able to see their house on the Web site. I think that more and more people are using it in larger scale searches to actually look for houses. That helps us as they then come to us better informed.

Is your Web site attached to realtor.com?

No, but it should be.

Do you or any members of your team do any telemarketing?

No.

What kind of mailings do you do?

Again, I really try to focus on high-quality, targeted mailings versus just mass mailings. As an example, I gave you an annual report on my market that I do each year, which I think gives me very good credibility. When I take a listing in one of the five markets I work in, I always do a color brochure. I always spend the money on color; it's very expensive, but I've found that's how people respond; that's how people identify who I am and what I'm all about. I'm consistent on the colors I use, burgundy versus blues versus greens. I'm very consistent on the look and consistent on the quality.

So you use continuity to help tie in the message about you and what you offer?

Yes, I want a repetitive message. I want people to identify me with quality representation. I know, and you know that people are not going to see this thing and read it. But as long as they glance at it and see the same message over and over, hopefully I've set up some kind of standard that they will remember.

Q

In your business plan, what percent of your gross commission income do you allocate toward marketing and advertising, and how do you track its effectiveness?

I set my advertising budget and my entire advertising plan at the beginning of the year. I know exactly what I am going to mail. I define how many mailings I want to do; whether they are annual reports, quarterly newsletters, or property brochures. Then, of course, it varies somewhat with the number of listings that I have. I really don't have a system to get direct feedback. When someone calls me, and the name is unfamiliar I will always ask him or her 'how did you get my name?' I usually find that about 50 percent of the time it's by referral and the other 50 percent of the time it's some sort of marketing. People will say, 'oh, I saw your name' or 'I received your flyer,' or something like that, so I know it's effective, but I honestly don't know how it's effective. I'm a real big believer in the blanket approach within my narrow and deep market; not mass-marketing, but consistent, effective marketing and advertising in the areas that I work.

Q

And do you allocate a certain percentage of your gross income as a limit?

I would say that it's probably been pretty consistently around 20 percent of my gross income.

Q

I'm hearing 18 to 20 percent pretty consistently.

Every year I'd like to reduce what I spend, but I haven't. That's not just advertising. So actually I think mine's less than some people because that figure includes gifts and my assistant.

Q

Oh, so that includes the cost of your assistant?

That's everything. I would say if you just look at my advertising, it's quite a bit less than that. I think that when most people talk about 20 percent, they're just talking about just what happens at the office while I'm including Christmas parties and everything. I would say that I'm closer to 15 percent. So I would say that compared to all my competitors, I'm probably less. But that's also because I don't have three or four assistants. I have one part-time assistant, and that's going to change, because I am in the process of adding a second part-time assistant. My philosophy is that my clients want to deal with me; they don't want me to pass them off to someone else. I find that to be very effective because people really get turned off when they hire a top performer, only to end up working all the time with their assistant instead.

I always worked that way, too, and, although I agree with you, I have seen people like Nikki Mehalic and David Vanneste build an effective business by marketing themselves as the lead person of a high-quality team.

My assistant is unlicensed, which is very unusual. She is literally my office manager.

Tell me what programs or systems you have in place to retain past clients and receive repeat and referral business from them.

Well, when I take a listing I always mail it to my past clients, not just the geographical area. That's number one. Any mailings that go out, including updates, always go to my past clients. I use Microsoft Outlook to keep track of clients and keep in touch with them. I try every quarter to contact everyone and just say 'Hi,' and try to put a good word in. I would say that the one thing that I could improve on is keeping in touch with clients. I think it's very critical, and I think I rest on my laurels too much. I mean, I find I'm so busy that that I don't always have enough time to keep in touch with old clients. I think it's probably pretty common.

Actually it's way too common, and it costs good agents a lot of money in lost business. About how many people are in your database?

I don't have as many as some people might think, maybe 250 people.

Q

And is that just past clients or is that past clients and target groups?

Oh, that's different. I'm sorry, that's a good question. For my actual database, I use an outside company called Marketing Designs. Marketing Designs does all my mailing for me. I don't know if they were around when you were here. They're a company in Belmont run by Jayne Geist, and basically I design the marketing pieces, and she puts them together. She works with me on all this stuff, all my brochures, everything. But the answer to your question is that I have about 5,500 people in my database.

Q

5,500 total? And that includes your various target marketing groups as well as your client base?

I was just thinking about that. My actual client base is much smaller.

Q

And you contact everyone in your database in some manner monthly?

Yes, I really think that it's important to keep in touch, and they seem to really like it.

Q

Does is vary according to the relationship that you have with them?

No, I've worried in the past about sending a $10 million flyer to someone I sold a $700,000 home to, but I really don't think that you lose credibility from that. I think your goal should be to keep your name and face in front of them. Remind them that you're out there; remind them that you can provide a service to them.

Q

Do you send them items of value or things of that nature on a regular basis to provide a service and to keep in touch, or is it strictly things like brochures? Items of value would be something that they can use in their every day life?

Well, that's the reason that I use the annual report, because I think that everyone wants to know what real estate values are. This area especially is not too much different. I think that California has such a phenomenal history of appreciation in real estate over the last 50 years that it's a common conversation with most people. If it isn't the stock market, it's real estate, and I think that's pretty common across the country. I think maybe more here than some places because we've had such tremendous appreciation with the Silicon Valley boom. So one of the reasons that I came up with the annual report is so that someone could actually have something to refer back to. I think that it's something that you actually keep and use as tool versus a color flyer that's fun to look at, but gets thrown away quickly.

Let talk about your team. You said your team consists of one part-time unlicensed assistant who is basically your office manager?

Yes, and I think that I'm probably going to be in the minority. I'm assuming that most of the people you talk to probably have at least two assistants with at least one being licensed.

A buyer's representative and a full-time assistant is quite common.

Sure, maybe one of the reasons my business expenses aren't as much as other people is because I'm not spending as much. I've been blessed with an extremely competent individual that I hired nine years ago, right after I started in the business. She's extremely bright, extremely capable of managing the paperwork, and understands both the business and the marketing. We came to a decision early on for her not to pursue her license. She really did not have an interest in it, which was good as I thought that I could retain her longer. One of my concerns about somebody that has a license is that someday they're going to go out on their own, once they see you making the money. The other idea is that I did not want to compete with her. I wanted her as a team member not as competition, and it's worked very well. I think that she's an integral part of everything I do with my clients. Everybody knows her; she's not a back-office person; she's a front-office person. People know her; she's interactive with my clients, and everybody really enjoys her. I think it's really important to find somebody, and I think it's worth paying the money for a really high-quality person, just so they can interact with your clients. It's worked very, very well. I've been very fortunate. Because there are certain times of the year that I'm rather overwhelmed, it can be

difficult to keep up with everything so I'm in the process of hiring someone else. I actually had a second assistant a year ago, and it didn't work
out. It was hard to find the same caliber of assistant that I have now. I
actually found somebody and am thinking of hiring her this week.

Q

> *Is that right? Now are you hiring a part-time person or are you
> hiring a full-time, licensed person?*

It would be a part-time person. She's not licensed, but she'll probably
get her license eventually. And I just think that she's great. It's taken
me a really long time to find someone who's really high-caliber to
come in and interact with clients.

Q

> *Let's talk now a little bit about company support. How much office
> space do you and your assistant occupy?*

We have a room that is about this size; this room is probably what, 12-
by-16 feet? I think it's made a tremendous amount of difference for
me going from a cubicle to a private office. You lose the direct inter-
action with other agents, but I think you can focus more on your
work. I also think the sense of privacy in the competitive environment
is something that is very important to me. It may not be important to
everyone, but I like to have private conversations and not have the
whole office overhear me. But I think more importantly the produc-
tivity has gone way up since we've moved to the private office. We've
kind of created our own environment here, and we're not interacting
with the noise and distractions that go on in the office space. I know
that traditional offices are cubicles, and that's how people interact, but
I've found private offices to be much more productive.

Q

> *What benefits does the company provide to you and your staff? Do
> you get any kind of extra advertising or supplies or company paid staff
> help from time to time?*

Zero.

Q

> *Zero; I thought that would be the answer.*

I think my manager does a very good job of treating everyone equally and on a level playing field. It's a very tough job to have top performers at different levels and make them all feel important. To her credit, I think that she does a good job keeping everyone happy, but I think that when you're working in the high-end, some of the buyers' and sellers' expectations are higher, and they feel they want to be treated differently. That can be challenging at times, because I have certain demands that maybe other agents wouldn't have, and it's nice to have your company and your manager support that. Coldwell Banker doesn't really do anything for the larger producers other than give them an office, that's probably the only perk that I get.

I would like to get your opinions and viewpoints of a couple of things. Producing the very high sales volume that you produce every year clearly sets you apart from the average real estate agent who would very much aspire to go where you are today. What do you do that is so effective and different from them? You've talked about a couple of things: number one going narrow and deep instead of broad and shallow; I guess I would coin a phrase and use that, but do you think that's a major issue?

Well, I think my ultimate goal is to make sure that my clients can walk away happy. That they feel that they chose the right agent and the transaction went well, and they were able to achieve the highest price and best terms for their property. I think that goal has served me very well, rather than just wanting to make the commission at the end of the day. I think that you have to be passionate about the business in order to accomplish high sales volume. But it's not just that;, I don't sit there and say, "gosh I want to make 'X' amount every year," or "I want this sales volume." I really have an inner desire to please my clients. I think that my personality, and any top salesperson's personality, really has to want to please; really has to want to aspire to make sure their clients are receiving the best service all the time. So, besides wanting financial success, that is one of the things that I feel has really motivated me. I really want to make sure that my clients are happy and satisfied, and I'll bend over backwards and do anything to achieve that end.

So you could say, maybe, that the reputation comes first, and the money follows?

I think so, because frankly if you can't keep your reputation consistent then it's very difficult to make money.

Q *Do you attribute part of your success to the design and consistency of your marketing programs and how effective they seem to be with various groups?*

I think that helps. Again, I decided to not use the shotgun approach and to really be methodical about how and where I market myself, whom I want as clients, and where I want my clients to come from. I think that being able to attract a certain client base to my business and not just take anybody who comes through the door has been an important factor in my success. Part of my success has also been having the discipline to say 'I don't want that client' or 'that type of listing would be detrimental to my business plan.' That's a very difficult thing to do. In the first five years, when I was establishing myself, it was difficult to turn down business, and it still is today, but I know that I can be much more productive and much more valuable to my clients when I stay focused. It's just as important for somebody to say no as it is to say yes.

Q *In your opinion what do you think is the single biggest benefit that you bring to your clients?*

I think that the knowledge of my market is number one. I really feel I know my market better than any other agent out there. I truly feel I understand the values; I understand not just property values, but I also understand the process of what buyers go through; I could go on and on, but you wanted a single answer.

Q *Give me a couple more, this is good stuff!*

Well, I think that you really have to step into your client's shoes to really be effective in sales. I think you really have to be passionate and understand where this client is coming from. It's about more than what they can spend; it's about what they really want to achieve. You know, one thing I really try to do is walk people through a property and really try to understand what they really want to end up with. I spent a long time learning about how each city works, how each municipality works. You know, like what the setbacks of a particular area like Atherton are. What are the height limits? What does is cost to build in this area? So, I am constantly talking to contractors, constantly talking to the city, really trying to get a better depth of understanding on how the process works. So if I show a client a piece of property, and the client gets stumped and says 'Gosh, you know this looks great, but we'd like a larger family room,' or 'We'd like a different design or different landscaping.' You can get creative if you've got an intimate knowledge of, and really understand the community you're working with. It's especially important to understand the building codes. The more that you know what's going on, the more value you bring to the transaction.

> ### *That is really good advice! Anything else?*

I'm thinking...

> ### *What about passion for what you do?*

Absolutely!, I think you have to be passionate about what you do. You have to be passionate to want to please, and I think that goes back to what I said earlier. The real carrot at the end of the stick for me is having the client happy, having them walk away and say 'Boy that was a great experience, that was a very positive experience.' That really motivates me, to keep my clients happy, and I think that there's nothing better that I can do than to walk away from the transaction and have my clients shake hands and say 'This was really well done, it was well received.'

> ### *Where do you see the residential real estate agent's role in the home-buying process going in the next several years?*

I know there are a lot of people who would think that everything is going to the Internet, and we're going to kind of be dissolved somehow, but I really feel that as long we can create value to our clients

we're going to be here for a long time. Again I think it's more important to have a very deep knowledge on not only your market as far as
inventory, but to also understand the depths of how things work and
the communities you work in. I really feel that the Internet and a lot
of the communication tools that we have, such as cell phones, pagers,
laptop computers, etc., will all be intricate tools and make us better,
more productive agents, but they won't replace us. I think it's going to
make the business more competitive, and it may narrow it down to
fewer agents. I think if someone's really passionate about the business
and really wants to please their clients, they will always be successful.

*I wanted to ask you earlier, do you have a team built? By that I
mean when I was in sales I had my favorite home inspector and termite
inspector, title person, escrow person, and everything. How important
do you think that is?*

I sure do have a team; I think it's very important for a number of reasons. The main thing is just efficiency. I think when someone calls and
wants to list their property, whether it's tomorrow or three weeks from
now, it's important to know what it takes and how you're going to do
it. I use the same inspectors that I've used now for probably three years
in a row, and there's no financial reward for me; just the satisfaction that
they're going to do a good job. I talk to each one of them individually,
and they are all very clear about why they're getting the business and
what kind of service to my clients it will take to keep the business. They
must do a very, very good job with my clients and provide them top
service. I feel that it is important to have a team of people. As I mentioned before, I set up what I call a 'Cornish Concierge Service.' I want
to go beyond just providing inspectors, I want to help clients prepare
their homes to go on the market so that they get the maximum price,
which I think that be very overwhelming for people.

Yes, especially in your higher-price homes.

That's right, and I think it's important for real estate agents to be forth-
right and have the guts to say 'Boy, that color's really unattractive' or
'Gosh, the landscaping needs to be improved.' If necessary, it's easy to
hire a professional person to stage the home, then they can be the bad

guy that tells the client what's necessary. I really think that people appreciate honesty, and I will often go in and say that I can either hire a stager, or I can just tell you what I think should be done. I think there are two types of agents: the agents that tell you what you want to hear and the agents who will tell you the truth. I fall into the latter category.

It's important for me to have a team of people to get a seller's house on the market looking it's best, a team that sees their home through the escrow, and a team for after the sale that efficiently handles property condition issues and things like that.

To me that sounds like real hands-on, value-added service from the time you meet the client to long after escrow.

Well, again it's a way I try to keep in contact with the client. If I can provide a service other than just the sale then I feel that I have done a really good job for them.

That's a great standard to work toward. What are the top three pieces of advice you can give to a real estate agent that wants to become a mega-producer?

I think it's really important to be disciplined. I think it's really important to set a goal and make a business plan that carefully identifies what areas one wants to work. That would be the most important thing, to identify ahead of time where you want to be successful. Once you've identified those areas then I think within that plan you have to incorporate what the detailed steps are that you are going to do to dominate that marketplace. So have a business plan, identify the areas that you want to work, identify how you're going to do it, and also identify a realistic time frame. I mean, it's not going to happen overnight. You have to give yourself time; you have to pace yourself. To earn people's respect takes a long time. And, then I think it's also important to really draw boundaries with people. It's very common in sales to get used and abused. The home purchase or sale process is a very emotional process for people, and they can sometimes become a bit abusive. You have to have a boundary and let them know when they have crossed it. You really should not compromise your values because once you do, that's when you get in trouble. That's when you become inefficient, and that's when you waste your time with people and your reputation can suffer.

Q

That is excellent advice. Is there anything else you'd like to tell the person reading this book?

I think that real estate is a wonderful business; it's an exciting business. If you like people and you love to please, if you like to get involved on a personal level with people, you couldn't ask for a better business to be in. To me there's nothing more personal than getting involved in the sale transaction of somebody's property, somebody's home, somebody's lifestyle, somebody's future. It's nice. I think it's a business that one has to be very passionate about. It's also important to have long-term goals and really work hard to be successful.

Appendices

Appendix A

Sample Marketing and Sales Materials from Mega-Producers

Nikki Mehalic
This is magnetic and stays very visible on people's refrigerators.

Nikki Mehalic
10445 N. ORACLE RD., SUITE 121 • ORO VALLEY • AZ 85737

PHONE	(520) 918-8840
TOLL-FREE:	1-888-825-8251
FAX:	(520) 825-8950
CELL:	(520) 349-4411
E-MAIL:	nikkiTRT@aol.com

www.tucsonluxuryestates.com

LONG REALTY COMPANY

Things To Do

Appendix A

Nikki Mehalic

This postcard was sent to a targeted group and represents that Nikki is a member of their community and is working in and for a specific community.

The Mehalic Team
"Having fun helping friends and neighbors!"

#1 in Oro Valley

Specializing in:
- Rancho Vistoso
- Honeybee
- Stone Canyon
- Coyote Ridge
- Moonridge
- Oro Valley
- Canada Hills

Areas of expertise:
- Lot sales
- New construction
- Custom homes
- Casitas
- Resales
- Golf properties
- Gated Communities

(520) 918-8840
(888) 825-8251 ext. 8840

LONG REALTY COMPANY

Visit our web sites-
www.vistosorealestate.com
www.tucsonluxuryestates.com

Eileen Herd   Nikki Mehalic, ABR   Debbie Valdes

Rancho Vistoso

96 W. Saddle Horse
MLS# 2220533

SEE VIRTUAL TOUR
www.realtor.com

LONG REALTY COMPANY

The Mehalic Team
10445 N. Oracle Road, Ste 121
Tucson, Arizona 85737

PRESORTED
STANDARD
US POSTAGE PAID
TUCSON, AZ
PERMIT NO 792

~HOME FEATURES~

- 4 Bedroom - 3 Bath
- 2,198 square feet
- US Home built
- Gorgeous Pool w/self cleaning
- Kitchen overlooking family room
- Corian counter tops
- Cul-de-sac location
- Close to elementary school
- Huge extended patio
- Lots of tile
- Ceiling fans
- 3-Car garage

Offered at
$249,900

LONG REALTY COMPANY

www.vistosorealestate.com

Represented by:
Nikki Mehalic
918-8840
Vistoso Specialist
#1 in Oro Valley

Russell Long

Glorious Hilltop Views.
This is a marketing and sales flyer that Russell uses on every listing, always showing the floor plan on the reverse side.

Glorious Hilltop Views

6021 E. Calle De Vita

This DRAMATIC 6180 sq.ft. Contemporary, located in the Catalina Foothills, offers 360 degree views, beautiful new carpeting and travertine... even more than can be imagined!

Christine and Russell Long
Tucson's #1 Real Estate Team
(520) 529-1116 Office
(888) 912-1116 Toll Free
1890 E. River Rd, Tucson, AZ 85718
View Virtual Reality: www.longrealty.com/longs
Long Realty Company

Appendix A

Russell Long

University of Arizona Men's Basketball Schedule.

This is a marketing postcard that is done annually and appeals to a local demographic that enjoys watching basketball.

2001 – 2002 UNIVERSITY OF ARIZONA
MEN'S BASKETBALL SCHEDULE

Schedule is tentative and subject to change

Day	Date	Opponent	TV	Location	Time PM
Sun	10/28	Pepsi Red-Blue Game		Tucson	3:00 MST
Sun	11/04	EA Sports All-Stars (EX)		Tucson	4:00 MST
(Coaches vs. Cancer IKON Classic)					
Thu	11/08	Maryland	ESPN	N.Y., N.Y.	9:00 EST
(Coaches vs. Cancer IKON Classic)					
Fri	11/09	Florida/Temple	ESPN	NY, N.Y.	TBA
Sat	11/17	Texas		Austin, Texas	TBA
Sun	11/25	Nike Elite (EX)		Tucson	7:00 MST
Sat	12/01	Kansas	CBS	Tucson	12:30 MST
Tue	12/04	Illinois	FSN	Phoenix, AZ	6:00 MST
Sat	12/08	Purdue *(Wooden Classic)*		Anaheim, CA	1:30 PST
Sat	12/15	Michigan State	CBS	East Lansing, MI	2:00 EST
Thu	12/20	Oregon State		Corvallis, OR	TBA
Sat	12/22	Oregon		Eugene, OR	6:00 PST
(Bank One Fiesta Bowl Classic)					
Fri	12/28	Pepperdine		Tucson	TBA
(Bank One Fiesta Bowl Classic) Consolation & Championship Game					
Sun	12/30	Valparaiso/West Virginia		Tucson	TBA
Fri	1/4	Oregon		Tucson	6:30 MST
Sun	1/6	Oregon State		Tucson	TBA
Thu	1/10	Washington State		Pullman, WA	TBA
Sat	1/12	Washington		Seattle, WA	7:00 PST
Thu	1/17	USC	FSN	Tucson	8:30 MST
Sat	1/19	UCLA	CBS	Tucson	12:00 MST
Wed	1/23	Arizona State	FSN	Tempe, AZ	8:30 MST
Sat	1/26	Connecticut	CBS	Tucson	11:00 MST
Thu	1/31	California		Berkeley, CA	7:30 PST
Sat	2/2	Stanford	FSN	Palo Alto, CA	5:00 PST
Thu	2/7	Washington		Tucson	6:30 MST
Sat	2/9	Washington State		Tucson	TBA
Thu	2/14	UCLA	FSN	Los Angeles, CA	7:30 PST
Sat	2/16	USC	ABC	Los Angeles, CA	3:00 PST
Wed	2/20	Arizona State		Tucson	7:30 MST
Thu	2/28	Stanford	FSN	Tucson	8:30 MST
Sat	3/2	California	CBS	Tucson	12:00 MST
Thu-Sat.	3/7 - 9	Pac-10 Tournament	FSN/CBS	Los Angeles, CA	TBA
Thu. - Sun.	Mar. 14-17	NCAA First & Second			
Thu. - Sun.	Mar. 21-24	NCAA Regionals			
Sat. - Mon.	Mar. 30-Apr. 1	NCAA Final Four			

UNITED WE STAND

David Vanneste

This refrigerator magnet is both a handout as well as an easy mailer. It is effective because it stays visible on the refrigerator.

(651) 481-6711

2002

JANUARY	FEBRUARY	MARCH
S M T W T F S	S M T W T F S	S M T W T F S
1 2 3 4 5	1 2	1 2
6 7 8 9 10 11 12	3 4 5 6 7 8 9	3 4 5 6 7 8 9
13 14 15 16 17 18 19	10 11 12 13 14 15 16	10 11 12 13 14 15 16
20 21 22 23 24 25 26	17 18 19 20 21 22 23	17 18 19 20 21 22 23
27 28 29 30 31	24 25 26 27 28	24 25 26 27 28 29 30
		31

APRIL	MAY	JUNE
1 2 3 4 5 6	1 2 3 4	1
7 8 9 10 11 12 13	5 6 7 8 9 10 11	2 3 4 5 6 7 8
14 15 16 17 18 19 20	12 13 14 15 16 17 18	9 10 11 12 13 14 15
21 22 23 24 25 26 27	19 20 21 22 23 24 25	16 17 18 19 20 21 22
28 29 30	26 27 28 29 30 31	23 24 25 26 27 28 29
		30

JULY	AUGUST	SEPTEMBER
1 2 3 4 5 6	1 2 3	1 2 3 4 5 6 7
7 8 9 10 11 12 13	4 5 6 7 8 9 10	8 9 10 11 12 13 14
14 15 16 17 18 19 20	11 12 13 14 15 16 17	15 16 17 18 19 20 21
21 22 23 24 25 26 27	18 19 20 21 22 23 24	22 23 24 25 26 27 28
28 29 30 31	25 26 27 28 29 30 31	29 30

OCTOBER	NOVEMBER	DECEMBER
1 2 3 4 5	1 2	1 2 3 4 5 6 7
6 7 8 9 10 11 12	3 4 5 6 7 8 9	8 9 10 11 12 13 14
13 14 15 16 17 18 19	10 11 12 13 14 15 16	15 16 17 18 19 20 21
20 21 22 23 24 25 26	17 18 19 20 21 22 23	22 23 24 25 26 27 28
27 28 29 30 31	24 25 26 27 28 29 30	29 30 31

1 Home Sold Every 3 Days!

www.vanneste.com

Appendix A

David Vanneste

This envelope is mailed out same day to every potential client that calls David.

David Vanneste
This folder and the four pages that follow are in the pre-mailer package.

How to Get Ready for your First Meeting with the Vanneste Group

1. Fill out the enclosed property information & utility sheets.

2. Fill out the enclosed Seller`s Questionnaire.

3. Have an extra key ready for our files.

4. Review the enclosed pre-listing packet on the process of buying and selling a home.

5. Write down any questions you may have for them when they arrive.

6. If available, have the blueprints to your house pulled out.

Appendix A

David Vanneste

This property information sheet asks for details on the property before the first meeting.

Vanneste's
Property Information Sheet

Owner Name _____ Work # ( ) _____ DOB _____

Spouse Name _____ Work # ( ) _____ DOB _____

Property Address _____ Mailing Address _____

Fax # ( ) _____ E-Mail Address _____

Cell # ( ) _____ Pager _____

What is the best way to reach you? _____

How did you hear of us? _____

Children:

Names _____ Ages _____ Birthdays _____

_____ _____ _____

_____ _____ _____

Pets (Type) _____

Would you prefer having open houses? Yes/ No Time/Day Preference: _____

What is most important to you in hiring a REALTOR? _____

What price range do you feel your home should sell for? _____

Schools: Elementary _____

                  Jr. High _____

                  High _____

Mortgage Information:

      1st Mortgage   Mortgage Holder _____

                              Loan Number _____

                              Phone Number _____ Approx Balance _____

      2nd Mortgage/Home Equity/Line of Credit (Even if there is a -Zero- balance!)

                              Mortgage Holder _____

                              Loan Number _____

                              Phone Number _____ Approx Balance _____

Association Information

    Name _____ Phone Number ( ) _____

    Contact Person _____ Fees _____

    Restrictions _____

Additional Home Improvements Since Occupying Home- BE SPECIFIC! INCLUDE DATES!

_____

_____

_____

Age of Roof _____ Installed by _____

    Warranties _____

Security System company _____ Phone # ( ) _____

    Owned/Leased? Monthly Cost _____ Police/Fire Monitored? _____

Central Vacuum System Yes/No Age _____ Warranty _____

Pool Age _____ Installed by _____ Warranties _____

    Any updates/maintenace, etc. _____

Any features/information you feel would be of interest to a new buyer?

_____

_____

Thank You For Your Business!

David & Donna Vanneste
Edina Realty
4570 Churchill Street
Shoreview, MN 55126
651-481-6711

Appendix A

David Vanneste

These forms are returned to David when the property is listed. They are used for escrow work and marketing.

UTILITY INFORMATION

Property Address _____

Type of Heating System _____

Water Company _____ Tank Owned or Rented? (Circle One)

    Average Water Bill $_____ / Month

Power Company _____

    Average Electric Bill $_____ / Month

    Average Gas Bill $_____ / Month

Cable Company _____

    Average Cable Bill $_____ / Month

Association Company _____

    Contact Name and Number _____

    Average Monthly Costs $_____

Garbage Service _____

    Contact Name and Number _____

    Average Monthly Costs $_____

Any other Services and their phone numbers that you feel would be helpful to potential buyers:

_____

_____

_____

SELLER'S QUESTIONNAIRE

Sometimes it's helpful for potential buyers to get the seller's perspective on the property. We'd appreciate your response to the following questions so that we can place this information in the brochure that is left in the property for buyers to view. **Please fill out and have it ready for your first meeting with David and Donna. Thank You!**

Why are you selling your home?

When you bought this house, what made this home a better choice than the rest?

What features have you enjoyed most in this home?

What features would you change if you were going to stay?

What improvements have you made during your ownership? (Please be specific)

Describe your yard and gardens since they are not visible during this season? (If applicable).

What characteristics of the area have you enjoyed most?

What inconveniences or problems exist with the area, if any?

Describe the people living in the neighborhood.

David Vanneste

This booklet is the first of several items that are pre-mailed to all sellers prior to meeting with David.

DAVID • DONNA
VANNESTE
GROUP

Pre-Listing Booklet

How the Vanneste Group Will Sell Your Home!

WE SELL A HOME EVERY 3 DAYS

651.481.6711
homes@Vanneste.com • www.Vanneste.com

Edina Realty inc.

Hugh Cornish

Hugh's Annual Review is an extremely comprehensive report on the previous year's real estate activity in the five cities in which he specializes. It is mailed to all property owners in those cities as well as a select group of venture capitalists, bankers, and other business people that Hugh knows.

HUGH CORNISH

2002 REAL ESTATE REVIEW

ATHERTON

MENLO PARK

PALO ALTO

PORTOLA VALLEY

WOODSIDE

Appendix A

2 0 0 2

REAL

ESTATE

REVIEW

For the cities of:

Atherton

Menlo Park

Palo Alto

Portola Valley

Woodside

February 2003

Dear Neighbor:

My name is Hugh Cornish. As many of you know, I am a residential real estate agent working out of the Menlo Park-El Camino office of Coldwell Banker. I specialize in representing both buyers and sellers in Atherton, Menlo Park, Palo Alto, Portola Valley, and Woodside.

Each year, as a service to my clients, I put together a Real Estate Review, summarizing and comparing the sales statistics for the year past to the previous two years. This has proven to be a useful tool, enabling my current and prospective clients to better understand market trends and residential property evaluations. I am delighted to share it with you, as well.

Please look over this review, and do not hesitate to give me a call if you have any questions. Happy New Year! I look forward to speaking with you soon.

Sincerely,

Hugh D. Cornish

HUGH CORNISH

#1 Agent in Menlo Park–
El Camino Office 2000, 2001, 2002

International President's Premier
Top 1% of all Coldwell Banker Agents

650-566-5353

hcornish@cbnorcal.com
www.hcornish.com

1000 El Camino Real • Menlo Park, CA 94025

About the Author

Bob Herd started his real estate career in early 1972 with a small company on the San Francisco Peninsula.

Although there was no real formal training programs or systems available in those days, Bob used some good initial training from his branch manager, his natural ability to interact with people, and his keen intuition about human nature to sell more than 60 homes his first and second years in the business and was awarded the coveted "TOP SALESPERSON" award from the real estate association that he belonged to in 1974.

Although Bob opened his own highly successful company in 1974, he still remained very active in sales, and under his training and guidance, one of his agents won the "TOP SALESPERSON" award from that same association every year for the next six years, except for 1979.

Over the course of his nearly 32-year career, Bob has been a salesperson, broker/owner, branch manager, and regional manager for some of the largest real estate companies in the San Francisco Bay area and Tucson, Arizona, but whether he was in a sales position or a nonselling senior management position, he has always maintained and nurtured in his associates a keen sense of the ever-evolving sensible, human-nature-based style of professionally handling the needs of customers and clients.

Bob maintains both a California and an Arizona broker's license and holds the Certified Residential Brokerage Manager (CRB), Certified Residential Specialist (CRS), and Graduate, Realtors Institute (GRI) designations. He is currently a branch manager for Coldwell Banker Success Southwest in Tucson, Arizona. You may reach Bob at (520) 240-2403 or by e-mail at rlherd@comcast.net.

Index

Index

Index

Index

1.) <u>Open Houses</u>

   Hold several at the same
   time (stagger a little) and
   date in the same area
   (food - beverage?)

2.) <u>Market Subdivisions and
   Builders</u>

3.) <u>Farm area</u>

4.) <u>Buyer Rep</u>

5. <u>Investors</u>
      A. Rentals
      B. Flips (buy fix up & sell)